CREATIVE
OPTIONS
TRADING

CREATIVE OPTIONS TRADING

JARROTT T. MILLER

Contemporary Books, Inc.
Chicago

Library of Congress Cataloging in Publication Data

Miller, Jarrott T
  Creative options trading.

  Includes index.
  1. Put and call transactions.   I. Title.
HG6041.M53 1979   332.6'45   79-50984
ISBN 0-8092-7192-3
ISBN 0-8092-7191-5 pbk.

Published by Contemporary Books, Inc.
180 North Michigan Avenue, Chicago, Illinois 60601
Manufactured in the United States of America
Library of Congress Catalog Card Number: 79-50984
International Standard Book Number: 0-8092-7192-3 (cloth)
                                   0-8092-7191-5 (paper)

Published simultaneously in Canada by
Beaverbooks
953 Dillingham Road
Pickering, Ontario L1W 1Z7
Canada

Contents

Preface

Sequels are often a tired rehash of some well-received theme that more often than not fail in the retelling. Only television seems to be able to successfully recast "Gunfight at the O.K. Corral" in one thousand and one variations.

Nonetheless, there are occasions, particularly in the rapidly evolving option field, when a continuation of a previous work is clearly justified. *Options Trading* (Contemporary Books 1975) was the first book to explore speculative techniques using the exchange traded security options that had been introduced the previous year by the Chicago Board Options Exchange. At that writing, the margin requirements for any transaction other than outright option purchase were quite restrictive. The market was quite new, its implications not fully understood, and the New York Stock Exchange and Federal Reserve rules were in the process of restructuring.

Those formative years are now behind us. Put options have been introduced, the margin requirements for all options have been intelligently rationalized, and the various strategies, both speculative and conservative, developed. The building blocks for the future are in place. The expansion of exchange traded security options will continue as both institutions and individuals increasingly use this financial instrument as an adjunct to their investment strategies. Certainly there will be further growing pains, most likely the product of either unscrupulous or inadvertent abuse. Maturing is always traumatic. Just the same, security options are well beyond adolescence and undoubtedly here to stay.

This book contains the same advice for the intelligent trading of options as recommended in *Options Trading*. Except now it applies to Puts as well as Call options. In addition, I will explore in considerable detail all of the various spreading strategies with *particular emphasis on* the impact of commissions, the risk/reward parameters associated with each, the worth and worthlessness of theoretical options valuation, and many valuable trading disciplines.

While the principal advantage of buying options is leverage combined with defined risk, options are also a wasting asset with a relatively short economic life. If an investor overinvests relative to his circumstances, he can suffer grievous financial injury.

Alternatively, selling options without an offsetting hedge position in either the underlying security (naked selling) or another option can have a high probability for profit. However, this tactic can also result in virtually unlimited margin calls in an extraordinarily volatile market.

The point is this: Every option strategy, from the simplest to the most sophisticated, entails risk in varying degrees. The most common investor mistake invariably involves taking risks that are disproportionate to one's resources. Sometimes this occurs because of naivete. Very often it results from overconfidence. In either case, the result can be the same—devastation. Such misfortune can be avoided through a combination of knowledge and judgment. This book will provide the knowledge. Each investor must supply his own wisdom. I can put the egg in your beer. You've got to spill your own foam.

Introduction

The options industry has had a long and invariably controversial history. Until just recently, dealings in options were private, or at least semiprivate, usually involving persons of wealth and financial sophistication. However, with the establishment of the Chicago Board Options Exchange, the first continuous marketplace for stock options, all the advantages of options are now easily within the grasp of the whole investing public.

Unfortunately, the financial press, in its coverage of the options business, has fostered a prejudicial attitude toward options buyers. "Option writers," it is said, are "either institutions or sagacious individuals of wealth acting wisely and prudently; options buyers," by the same argument, are "rank speculators, gamblers, or at least uninformed fools." By this logic, the dynamic growth of the options business is attended by a disproportionate increase of horses' asses among the public.

Of course, the truth of the matter is that many option speculators are artless wishful thinkers who persist in the hope of getting a free lunch. Back at the turn of the century, they disgorged their millions in the bucket shops. Bucket shops were the illegitimate face of the legitimate Member Firm Brokerage Houses. A handy storefront, a little money spent on decor and the wages of a few clerks—and an operator was in business.

When a customer walked into a bucket shop, the operation looked like the real thing. The clerks would be busy changing the current prices of stocks listed on a large blackboard. A ticker tape clacking out the price quotes from the New York Stock Exchange would be close at hand. The tape and the board were the center of interest for the lounging observers. As soon as the customer decided which stock he wanted to "purchase," he would place an order at the cashier's cage and put up 10 percent of the price, in theory borrowing the balance. He received a receipt noting the current price of the stock, the number of shares, and the amount of margin money paid. The order to buy went into the wastebasket, i.e., it was "bucketed." In fact, the customer was betting that the stock would go up and the house was betting against him. If it did go up, the customer would present his receipt to the cashier and receive the new price of his shares less commissions and the amount of his "loan." Should the price decline, the customer would get a call to put up more margin. If he failed to do so (and about all customers did), his position would be wiped out and the shop would keep his money. He had lost his bet.

By dealing with bucket shops, the speculator could at least limit his risk. The bucket shops never came after his bank account for more margin. They just pocketed his original bet along with those of thousands of other crapshooters. On the other hand, if he happened to make a killing, he might also find his favorite bucket shop had reverted into an empty storefront overnight, the operator having taken the night train to the next town.

Speculation has always been with us and always will be. Sometimes it serves an economic and social purpose, other times not. However, for the individual the most important distinction is whether his speculations are stupid or wise. There is a great body of intelligent speculators who are aware of the potential advantages of buying options compared to other forms of out-and-out gambling in the stock market. This book is addressed to these prudent speculators and would-be speculators.

No aspect of financial analysis has been so ignored as that of speculating with options. The industry has blithely assumed that the population consists of an inexhaustible supply of suckers who will buy whatever is offered. However, a healthy, sturdy options industry will only prosper when all the participants are equally well informed. If the sheep don't get smart, the wolves will never go hungry.

CREATIVE OPTIONS TRADING

1

The History of Options

The business section of your local bookstore will seldom have less than three and often many more titles dealing with options. The financial newspapers and periodicals are equally well stocked with advertisements for options services. Invariably, the thrust of all this effort is to make you more knowledgeable about *writing* options. The purpose of this book is to point out the advantages of *speculating* with exchange traded options. Techniques for selecting the most highly leveraged and least risky options will be disclosed. The strategies of outright purchase, option trading, naked selling, and option hedging will be discussed. All in all, this book should benefit the occasional speculator, the serious trader, and even the most intractable option writer. Before getting enmeshed in the specifics, let's take a brief look at the evolution of the option.

Few realize that options have been used in commerce since biblical times. For the student, their history is fascinating. For the more practical minded, a knowledge of the antecedents of our present options business will point out some of the more imaginative ways in which these remarkable versatile tools can be used.

Aristotle wrote in his *Politics* that the ancient philosopher Thales made a fortune through the clever use of options. Being a careful observer as well as a thinker, Thales concluded that the next year's olive crop in Miletus would be very bountiful. Since a philosopher's pay was no better then than today, he sought to capitalize on his judgment and leverage his funds. He procured options on virtually every olive press in the district for the next harvest season and effectively "cornered the market." When the bumper crop arrived, he leased out the presses at exorbitant rates and thus secured his fortune.

The option with which Thales dealt was a good skeleton but lacked some of the flesh of its more refined offspring. Basically, an option is a right. The option seller grants a right to do something. The option buyer pays money to the seller to receive that right. The money that changes hands is called the option money or option premium. In commerce, the right is usually the right to buy or sell an article at a price agreed upon at the time the option is entered into. Usage has established that the name of the option is determined by the nature of the right viewed from the buyer's standpoint. If the buyer pays his option money so that he can take something from the seller at the agreed upon price, the option is termed a Call. If the buyer's right is to give something to the seller, the option is called a Put. (Interestingly enough, in contemporary England, Calls are referred to as Takes and Puts as Gives.) The last element of an option is one of time. Since a specific amount of money is paid for the option, the option normally only lasts for a specific length of time. This is also agreed to when the option is bought. If the option buyer chooses not to exercise his right, the right will expire. The option seller or grantor is richer by the premium. Presumably, the option buyer chose to forfeit his option right because of some other economic justification.

The first sophisticated use of options in history occurred during the legendary tulip-bulb craze in 17th century Holland.

In the 1630s the Dutch became so enamored of tulips that the prices of the bulbs began to rise by leaps and bounds. At the onset those in the trade used options for hedging. A dealer with a forward sales commitment would buy sufficient Calls to assure that he would have the necessary bulbs at a set price when he had to deliver the physical product. On the other hand, tulip-bulb growers would buy Put options to guarantee a market at a set price for their product. However, as the mania really took hold, speculators rushed to buy Calls as the most profitable vehicle to wealth for the least amount of capital. As prices spiraled upwards, the owners of the Calls made more money than the speculators who bought the bulbs themselves. Virtually all commerce in Holland ceased, save the trading in tulip bulbs and related paper.

Legend has it that a visiting sailor triggered the "coup de theatre" by inadvertantly lunching on a $10,000 tulip bulb, thinking it to be an onion.

This instance of folk wisdom might have put the inflated prices into perspective. More likely, the reality that the handful of frenzied spendthrifts willing to pay a king's ransom for a single bulb could hardly digest the hundreds of thousands of tubers that Holland grew caused complete disintegration of the trade. The speculators who had spent their life savings buying Calls on the economically useless bulbs were ruined. Put writers, either unable or unwilling to pay out their fortunes for the bulbs Put to them, went bankrupt. Options, so intimately involved in the craze and the collapse that followed, acquired a bad name that is still with us today.

In the United States, trading in Puts (contracts to sell stock at a fixed price for a set period of time) and Calls (contracts to buy stock at a specified price for a set time interval) had been used by sophisticated and professional traders since the inception of the securities market. However, it was not until the 1860s that options trading became widespread. One man, Russell Sage, became the propelling and dominating force in the options business.

RUSSELL SAGE

Sage arrived on Wall Street with a hoard of capital accumulated from a variety of commodity and shipping enterprises. He promptly put his money to work at very profitable interest rates. The insatiable demand for capital and loans during this period of the nation's commercial expansion soon made him an extremely wealthy man. One of his largest sources of income came from lending money to great personages for their various stock acquisitions and manipulations.

Sage's career as a banker was interrupted when he was indicted in 1869 for lending money at usurious rates. Although defended by several prominent politicians who had benefited over the years by his loans, he prudently decided to disguise the "same old business" with a new face. Sage was a master speculator who saw great opportunity where lesser men saw nothing. Truly, he could have sold long johns in the Fiji Islands.

His first innovation was the "conversion," an invention of true genius. When approached by a client who wanted to borrow money to buy stock, Sage accommodated his client using options, or "privileges" as they were then known. First he would demand a *free* Put from the eager client. Next he would purchase 100 shares of the object stock, and then in turn *sell* a Call to the client. Should the stock decline, he could Put the shares to the client and so be protected. Should the stock rise, the client, by exercising his Call at the lower option price would derive the full benefit. Regardless of the fate of the stock, Sage could neither make nor lose capital. His profit came from selling the Call, and the State of New York had no usury laws governing the sale of Calls.

The client, by giving a Put and buying a Call, had all the advantages and attendent risks of owning the stock outright. Obliquely, Sage still maintained his usurious lending business; his clients achieved their speculative purposes; and the attorney general of New York had to seek other, less wily game.

Sage's inventive turn didn't stop with conversions. He then went on to the "straddles" and "spreads." A straddle is a combination of a Put and a Call, each having the same striking price. A spread straddle is a straddle wherein the component Put and Call are at different striking prices. Sage devised most of the elements of the modern options business. His contributions earned him the title of "Father of Puts and Calls" and, alternatively, "old Straddle."

Having forged the tools, Sage was no slouch in their profitable deployment. However, he shunned the public eye. Many of his deals depended upon the confidentiality of the transactions for their success. Consequently, some of the more famous and infamous market operators received credit for spectacular manipulations that rightfully belonged to Sage. Sage never took umbrage. He was fully satisfied with profit.

Russell Sage, like all men at the forefront of an enterprise that attracts public scrutiny, was quick to justify his activities in the most favorable light. He first revealed that he "had entered the occult business of option writing to help out small brokers who wished to operate on his huge capital."[1]

One might question Sage's espoused generosity considering that he could exert substantial influence on the market. If a particular stock's price movement was not to his benefit, he certainly had the wherewithal to make the price do his bidding.

Secondly, Sage contended that "since the purchasers of said Puts, Calls, straddles, etc., could never lose more than the premium cost of those options, he [Sage] provided the 'poor man' with a chance to profit from the price movements of 'blue chips' in the same manner as the rich man who could maintain a margin account—only without any risk over and above the option's cost to the purchaser."[2]

Sage's observation of the facts was absolutely correct, although his implication that he wanted to benefit the "poor man" had more than a small touch of hypocrisy.

Sage also recommended certain strategies for using options.

---

1. Paul Sarnoff, Russell Sage: The Money King (New York: Astor-Honor 1965), p. 237.
2. Ibid.

For all the color that surrounded his life he was above all a very conservative, though unorthodox, financier. He seldom really took risks. By writing options on stocks he virtually controlled, he avoided risk. His adroit handling of the conversion was foolproof. It was Russell Sage, the master, who stated that the only sensible way to trade a market was to use a Call to protect a short sale and a Put to protect a long position.

The days of the "lawful" manipulators have come and gone. This isn't to say that there aren't any unscrupulous entrepreneurs still around looking for an opportunity. As long as wealth is portable (e.g., currency, bank balances, bonds, stocks, etc.), as opposed to the more cumbersome varieties (e.g., cattle, wives, stone wheels, etc.), some shrewd fellow will find a way to convey the public's money into his pocket, the law be hanged. Witness the escapades of Tony De Angelis, Billy Sol Estes, Bernie Cornfeld, Robert Vesco, et al.

Over-the-Counter Options

2

In Sage's day, the option market was a completely private affair. The option writer and the option buyer sat down face to face and individually negotiated the terms. As the interest in options became more widespread, an over-the-counter (OTC) market was formed. This market for the most part supplanted the need for face-to-face negotiations and therefore enabled buyers and writers in different parts of the country to make deals. Two developments made this possible. The first grew out of the force of custom. Convention had established that a single option would always cover 100 shares, even though any theoretical number was possible. Also, the length of time the option would run was generally standardized at thirty-day, sixty-day, ninety-day, six-month-and-ten-day, and one-year intervals. The expiration date was set at one of these intervals from the day the agreement was made. These conventions greatly simplified the number of problems that had to be resolved in coming to terms.

The second development was the emergence of a trade group

that specialized in options. Practically all orders for the purchase and sale of OTC options were executed in New York by members of the Put and Call Brokers and Dealers Association, Inc. This association, which consisted of approximately twenty members was a self-regulated organization that dealt exclusively in options. Each option firm acted as a broker, or middleman, to bring an agreeable buyer and seller together. Income resulted from transaction commissions as well as any profits from the option inventory maintained to service customers.

Most importantly, each option was guaranteed by a member firm of the New York Stock Exchange. Since an option buyer pays cash when he buys an option contract, this side of a contract needs no assurances. On the other hand, the seller (or writer) of the option promises to perform an obligation (either buy or sell 100 shares of stock) any time during the duration of the option in return for the money he receives (the premium) for the option. The member firm (almost all medium-to-large brokerage firms are members of the NYSE) guaranteed that its customer, the customer who wrote the option, would perform on his contract whether it was profitable or not. This guarantee of performance was the hinge pin between reputable business and the bucket shop. In order to protect this guarantee, the brokerage houses kept a close eye on the customers they allowed to write options, and usually have fairly stringent capital requirements for such customers.

Some years ago one major brokerage house allowed too many undercapitalized customers to write naked Call options, i.e., writing Calls without buying the underlying stock. The market subsequently rose to such an extent that many of the customers refused to buy in the stock to deliver to the option holders. The house that had guaranteed the options stood good on the transactions, but the capital drain was so severe that it was forced into a shotgun merger with a financially sound competitor. The financial criterion for option writers has since been substantially upgraded.

With the emergence of the exchange-traded option on two hundred and nineteen stocks, the importance of the OTC option market has definitely waned. There are currently only three active Put and Call Broker-Dealers doing any appreciable business. Nonetheless, an astute investor sometimes uncovers an attractive situation on which listed options are not available. In such an instance, the OTC market is the only, even if somewhat diminished, alternative. And as such, the imaginative investor must become familiar with the mechanics of its operation.

As already stated, an OTC option contract is individually negotiated between buyer and seller with a Put and Call Broker-Dealer acting as an intermediary. Generally, the strike price or price at which the option is set is the price of the underlying stock on the day the option contract is entered into, although in some instances the option contract might specify some other strike price. A Call where the strike price is below the prevailing underlying stock price, or a Put where the strike price is above the current stock price, is called an "in-the-money" option. A Call where the strike price is above the stock price or a Put where the strike price is below the stock price, is an "out-of-the-money" option. If the contract is a straddle (one Put and one Call on the same stock), the strike price will be the same for each leg of the double option. A variation of the straddle is the OTC "spread," where each component of the double option has a different strike price.

The price of the option, or option money (usually referred to as the premium) is the principal bargaining point over and above the duration of the option. When a buyer is interested in an option on a particular stock, he used to be able to check ads in the *Wall Street Journal, Barron's,* or the *New York Times* to see what was offered by the option dealers themselves. With the contraction of OTC option activity, the main source of information is now his stock broker who will query the remaining option dealers for him. Since not all brokerage houses are active in OTC options, he should obviously be doing business only with a house that is option oriented. Most NYSE member firms are. When a buyer gets a quote from his broker, he can either accept it or counter with a lower bid.

These negotiations usually take place over the phone or teletype. In some cases, the broker's Put and Call department can haggle with a Put and Call dealer who is willing to sell the option out of his inventory. In other cases, either the broker's Put and Call department or the Put and Call dealer will be in direct contact with an investor willing to write the option. If the prospective buyer thinks the price is too high and counters with a lower bid, he has no assurance that it will be accepted. In fact, if too much time is lost in fiddling, the original offer to sell the option might be withdrawn. This is particularly true if the option desired is very popular, or events are moving rapidly. Such are the problems of trying to put deals together over long distance.

As a guideline, option writers seek an annualized return from their option writing activities of from 25 to 40 percent. As one might expect, the writer demands a higher return, and therefore, a higher premium, for writing on the more volatile speculative issues, and will settle for a lower return for writing on the less volatile, less risky investment grade stocks. The overall tone of the market and the underlying stock in particular will have a bearing on option prices. In a falling market, the prices of Calls tend to decline and the prices of Puts tend to rise. The converse is true in rising markets.

Since options are always on 100 shares of stock, the prices are again, by convention, quoted in points per share under option. As an example, a six-month-and-ten-day Call option on Coldwell Banker stock at 29 might be offered at 3½. That means that the Call would cost the buyer 3½ per share or $350.00 for the whole 100-share option. You will also note that all fractional prices are always stated in multiples of ⅛ point, just as are the prices on the underlying stock. If the price is low enough, ¹⁄₁₆ of a point is sometimes used. Since commissions are involved, the option seller receives ⅜ of a point less than what the buyer pays: ⅛ point goes to the buyer's stock broker, ⅛ goes to the broker's Put-and-Call dealer, and ⅛ point goes to the seller's stock broker.

An OTC option confers virtually all the benefits of stock ownership on the holder of the option. If the stock on which the holder has an option were to split two for one, the option terms would be appropriately modified, i.e., each option would increase from 100 shares to 200 shares. Similarly, if a dividend is paid on the optioned stock, the strike price of the option is reduced by a like amount. For the holder of a Call on the stock, the effect is to give the dividend to the option holder if he exercises the option. Just as the short seller is liable to pay any dividends to the person from whom he has borrowed the stock to sell short, the reduction of the strike price for a Put holder serves the same purpose. Of course, if the options are not exercised, the Call holder doesn't receive the dividend and the Put holder doesn't have to pay it since the adjustment is made via the alteration of the strike price.

This subject brings up the whole topic of what to do with the option once you own it. As is true with most securities, the disposition is frequently more critical than the acquisition. With OTC options, this problem is even more complex because of the ephemeral life of the option and the very limited resale possibilities.

The only time an option buyer can be assured of a resale market for an OTC option is just before its expiration. If the option is worthless because it has no intrinsic value (say, a Call on GM at $80 when the common is at $50), the brokerage house with whom the buyer does business will buy the option from him for $1. The broker performs this as a service for his customer. Obviously, he has no other reason. The customer, by disposing of his worthless option at some price, can clearly establish the date of his capital loss for tax purposes.

More happily, should the option owner's judgment have been sound and the option approach expiration with a profit, he has two alternatives. Let's take the case of a speculator who, having bought one Call on Natomas at $45 for $525, gleefully watches Natomas bounce to $55 as his Call approaches expiration. At this point, the Call has an intrinsic value of $1,000. He can exercise his Call (buy NOM at $45) and then resell the stock on the open market at $55. He will pay a commission of approximately $85 to his broker to buy the 100 shares at $45 and then pay another commission of approximately $85 when he resells his 100 shares at $55. Consequently, the whole cost of the option transaction is the cost of the $525 plus the two commissions ($85 plus $85 or $170) for a total of $695. Since the gross profit is ($55 minus $45) times 100 shares or $1,000, the net is $305. This is a return of 58 percent on the original investment of $525.

The transaction would be classified as a short-term capital gain for tax purposes since the stock was purchased and sold the same day. The cost of the option and subsequent commission costs would be added to the purchase price basis of the stock. One *could* get a long-term capital gains treatment by exercising the option and then holding the stock for more than one year before selling it, assuming, of course, that NOM didn't drop back to $45.

The alternative to exercising the option to realize the profit would be to sell the "in-the-money" option outright. Here again, the customer's broker will usually buy the option from his customer. If the option is a profitable Call held longer than one year, selling the option itself at a profit will establish a long-term capital gain for the option holder. The broker will then in turn exercise the option and charge the customer the same two commissions as if he had done the job himself. The only advantage is the tax benefit. However, this advantage is quite meaningful if the option is a Put, since this technique is the only way that a long-term capital gain can be realized from anything resembling a short sale. Unfortunately, the recent change in the long-term holding period and the scarcity of option sellers willing to take a one year exposure severely limit this opportunity.

The foregoing is not meant to imply that there is *no* secondary resale market for OTC options. A dealer will occasionally buy profitable options that still have considerable life left. However, this limited resale market is not large and is pretty much confined to the most popular options. These options are in turn resold as "special" options by the dealer. In those cases where the original option buyer has a profit and resells to a dealer, the commission cost is only the same ⅜ of a point normally charged when the option was first written. This is quite a cost advantage when compared to the double commission cost charged on the underlying stock to exercise and resell. Nonethless, you should *never* buy an OTC option with the idea that you will be assured of a resale opportunity.

There is one other special situation in which there is a possibility of resale of a profitable option. If the option customer has had a long and favorable experience with his broker, the broker will under certain conditions, and only as a service to the customer, buy a profitable *Put* option from the customer. (Unfortunately, this service does not apply to Calls.) The broker then "converts" the Put. He buys 100 shares of the underlying stock and sells a Call. Because the public interest is always skewed towards the long, optimistic buy side, Calls usually command a better price than Puts. In buying the cheaper Put and selling the more expensive Call, there is sufficient money left over to pay the interest charges on the money borrowed to buy the 100 shares of stock. The broker is now long 100 shares of stock, long one Put, and short one Call. The broker is completely secure in his conversion. If the stock drops, he can put the stock he bought to the original Put seller and the Call will go unexercised. If the stock price rises, he will let the Put expire and deliver the stock over to the Call buyer. The broker is completely hedged. This is the same technique that Russell Sage used, except that Sage got his Puts free instead of paying for them.

However, when the interest rates on money are at the 10 percent level, very few brokers will do any conversions because the difference between the Put and Call prices is not enough to pay the interest charges on the money borrowed to buy the stock.

Given that a resale market cannot be counted on except close to the expiration date, and only rarely any other time, the usual method of capturing profit is by exercising the option. Under the terms of the option agreement, the option can be exercised at *any* time during its life. Most option buyers, however, tend *not* to exercise until the last minute. Their rationale is that they bought time and don't want to squander any of their option by premature exercise. Often they will hold on even though their best judgment tells them that the underlying stock's move has peaked out.

The OTC options business grew enormously after the days of Russell Sage. According to a 1961 Securities and Exchange Commission (SEC) study, sales of options increased from 0.49 percent of the NYSE volume in 1943 to 1.12 percent in 1960. In June of 1959, the number of options outstanding (presently called open interest, a term borrowed from the commodities futures industry) covered some 3,700,00 shares of stock.

Several developments have occurred in recent years that have dramatically heightened the interest and enlarged the scope of options trading even further. The first was the introduction of the down-and-out option. The second, and most important, was the establishment of the Chicago Board Options Exchange (CBOE).

DOWN-AND-OUTERS

Early in the 1970s, several brokerage houses (Goldman Sachs, Donaldson, Lufkin & Jenrette, Bear Stearns, and Oppenheimer) began marketing a new kind of option. In Street jargon, it was called the down-and-outer. The idea behind presenting this new product was to offer an option that would give a "fairer shake" to the buyer.

The first of the special features of the down-and-outer (the proper technical name is "special expiration price option") benefits the writer. These options have an *expiration price* as well as the usual expiration date. In the case of a Call, if the price of the common under option falls to the expiration price, the Call automatically expires. If the option is a Put (some brokerage houses do make a market in up-and-outer) and the price of the optioned stock advances to the expiration price, the

Put expires. The purpose is to let the option writer off the financial hook if his underlying position deteriorates. The Call writer is not required to hold a plummeting stock, nor is a Put writer obliged to hold a skyrocketing short. With the option automatically cancelled, the writer can bail out and completely free his capital as well.

As an example, if a six-month-and-ten-day down-and-out Call were bought on a $40 stock, the expiration date would be six months and ten days hence. The expiration price would be around $36. The usual "out" price is 10 percent below the strike price for a Call and 10 percent above for a Put. If the stock never fell to $36, the option would expire in a little over six months. Otherwise sooner.

What advantage would induce buyers to purchase options which could possibly expire overnight? The greatest advantage of all—cheapness. Down-and-outers are sold for just about half the price of the usual OTC option. Whereas the cost of a six-month option usually amounts to 20 percent of the cost of the underlying stock, down-and-outer can be bought for a little more than half that amount.

Low cost is not the only feature used to attract buyers. These options have a rebate feature that amounts to a kind of resale market. If the buyer chooses to exercise the option before the expiration date, he will receive a pro rata share of his option money back. On a six-month option, this would amount to a $1/6$ rebate per month. Thus, if the option were exercised at the end of one month, $5/6$ of the option cost would be rebated; if at the end of three months, $1/2$ would be rebated. Consequently, it can be advantageous to exercise an unprofitable option just to get part of the option cost back. A little salvage on a bad option is a lot better than a dead loss.

The brokerage houses that write and market the down-and-outers and up-and-outers have deliberately chosen to maintain a very low profile. Only favored clients are solicited for the business. For subtle schizophrenic reasons, the houses that introduced these special options don't really want to be very closely associated with the options business. The rationale seems to be that what is respectable with a high-class clientele is disreputable with the public. Since antiquity, the most successful madames have operated their businesses on just such a basis.

THE CHICAGO BOARD OPTIONS EXCHANGE

Established in April 1973, as an offshoot of the Chicago Board of Trade, the world's largest commodity futures trading market, the CBOE has been the most significant innovation in options since Russell Sage's day.

In November 1973, the sales volume of options, both OTC and listed, had increased to more than 6 percent of the New York Stock Exchange volume. The new business on the CBOE accounted for the lion's share of this startling increase. By March 1974, the CBOE monthly trading volume of equivalent shares had further increased to 33.6 million shares, equal to 11 percent of *all* the shares traded during the month on the NYSE. By May 1974, this figure had bounded to 121.2 percent of the equivalent NYSE volume.

With such success, competition was quick to respond. The American Stock Exchange started an options exchange followed by the Philadelphia, the Pacific, and finally the Midwest Stock Exchange. The New York Stock Exchange is also quite interested, but there are formidable lobbying pressures against such a venture both within and without government. Be that as it may, the options market has continued to thrive. The *Wall Street Journal* estimated that in 1978 the option trading volume for its 219 optionable stocks was equal to 79 percent of the total NYSE volume on *all* of its 1800 plus stocks. When the Securities and Exchange Commission finally lifts its 1977–1979 moratorium on listing new optionable stocks, it's not unreasonable to expect that options volume might well surpass that of all listed common stocks. The stepchild might outgrow the parent.

3

Exchange-Traded Options

As has been pointed out in the previous chapter, one of the most serious disadvantages (from the buyer's standpoint) of OTC options is the virtual absence of a resale market. If a man holds an option that has considerable life remaining, his two alternatives are either to exercise the option or to lock in the profit by trading against the option. In either instance, the option holder must come up with additional cash to finance the operation and must also pay substantial commission costs based on the higher price of the underlying shares. It is only infrequently that he can just sell his profitable option outright to capture profit with no further financial outlay.

By the same token, an *unprofitable* option with substantial life still remaining can seldom be unloaded to another buyer. The premium paid for the option is valueless to anyone other than the original buyer. Buying OTC options is a great deal like some of the "one-decision" stocks that many of the large institutions have bought themselves into. Once you've got it, you're stuck with it unless it makes money. Their holdings are so large that they can only sell into a rising market. In a dull or down market, there are simply no buyers for a major block. There's no way to cut a loss.

On the other hand, the option writer has much more latitude. If he sold a Call against a stock he owns and the stock heads south, he can sell the stock and go "naked." While he must leave margin money in his account to secure the still-outstanding Call, with the stock dropping, the Call will most likely expire unexercised. If the option writer writes a Put against an existing short sale and the price advances, he can likewise cover his short and use cash to secure the outstanding, potentially worthless Put. In these ways, writers can more readily limit losses and safeguard their capital.

What this boils down to is that, historically, the option market has been biased for the writer and loaded against the buyer. The odds favor a seller writing against a diversified portfolio. A buyer really needs uncommon skill, luck, and timing to hit enough jackpots to pay off the myriad of complete losses and return a profit. But history shows that very few men acquired their wealth through buying conventional options. Sage made more money selling options to Gould than Gould made with the options he bought.

FUNDAMENTALS OF LISTED OPTIONS

And then along came the Chicago Board Options Exchange. Conceived by the Chicago Board of Trade in 1969, approved by the Securities and Exchange Commission in February 1973 for a "pilot operation," the CBOE began trading on April 26, 1973, in Call options on sixteen carefully selected stocks. On that day, 911 option contracts exchanged hands. Less than nine months later more than 15,000 contracts per day were trading. In 1978, approximately 55 million contracts changed hands on the five options exchanges with the CBOE still dominating the trade volume with roughly 34 million contracts. Listed options have clearly stolen the OTC option market's thunder.

Investors and speculators alike had many misgivings about the CBOE before it opened its doors. The multiple and fixed exercise prices, and the fixed expiration dates four times a year, were thought to be too confusing. Trading in Call options alone (trading in Puts began at a later date) was considered to be too one-sided to be practical, especially when options on only sixteen stocks were available. Additionally, many skeptics disdained any association of the new options market with the giant, old commodities market. They apparently felt that the institutional clients who are most often option writers either would not or could not participate in a venture so related.

The gloomsayers seem to have been driven from the field. The volume and open interest on the exchange have grown to such an extent that the trading facilities were jampacked only eight months after the doors were opened. The phenomenal acceptance of this new market stems from a need very capably satisfied.

Listed options were designed for one prime objective—*marketability*. To achieve this quality, the expiration dates and strike prices on the options have been standardized. Neither changes as the price of the common fluctuates or as time passes. Standardizing all the salient option terms, save the price, established the basis for liquidity. The ability to buy, sell, or resell in a public auction has opened a whole new financial realm. An option bought one day can be sold the next, or the day after, or any day up until the expiration date. The prices of the options, the trading volume, and open interest are quoted every day in the *Wall Street Journal*. Instantaneous prices are available during the trading hours from any broker. Not only are the option exchanges *resale* markets for options, they are *public* markets. The sophisticated and unsophisticated, the professional and the amateur, the wise and the foolish may all participate.

All exchange-traded options have fixed expiration dates. When the CBOE first opened, there was only one expiration "cycle," starting with three-month intervals after January. Thus the January "cycle" was January, April, July, and October. As additional underlying stocks were introduced, some were put on a February, May, August, and November cycle. The last batch of stocks introduced in 1977 were put on a March, June, September, and December cycle. The purpose of spreading the months across the whole year was to average out some of the hectic trading often associated with an expiring option month.

While there are obviously four expiration months in each annual cycle, only three are ever traded at the same time. Using the January cycle, on the trading day after the Januarys stop trading the Octobers will be introduced. Thus the longest option available can only be nine months and it is only around for a day or two after a new expiration month option has started trading. The shortest option that can be bought is one bought on the day it expires. Of course, just before an option month expires, the longest option available is one for six months. In essence, an option's life is measured from the day it is bought until the day it expires. Every waning day diminishes all listed options by one day.

An option that has been purchased can be either sold or exercised on any trading day until the third Friday of its expiration month. An option that was sold can also be bought back. That's what exchange-traded options are all about. This feature of resaleability in a regulated secondary marketplace is what has stirred the imagination and enthusiasm of investors. All trading is halted at 2:00 P.M., CST, on that third Friday and the owner of an option, either a Put or a Call, must notify his broker if he wishes to exercise his option by 4:30 P.M., CST, on the same day.

Table 1 depicts a stock with its full spectrum of options. Both the stock and the option prices are real. However, because option

Table 1   Option Prices on XYZ @ 34¾

Strike Price	February (2 months)		May (5 months)		August (8 months)	
	Calls	Puts	Calls	Puts	Calls	Puts
40	⅜ R	5⅜	1¼	5¾	2⅛	6¼
35	1⅞	1⅝	3¼	2⅝	4⅜	3⅜
30	5⅝	¼	6¼	⅞	7⅛	1¼

prices as related to the common stock price will vary according to demand, the economic environment, and investor psychology, I have chosen to substitute the name of XYZ.

I would suggest that the reader turn down the page corner because we'll be referring to Table 1 quite frequently.

The strike prices (also known as exercise prices) aren't created out of the blue. When an underlying stock is first admitted for options, the starting strike prices usually bracket the stock price. For example, a $26 stock would have options with 25 and 30 strike prices. Were the stock to subsequently advance to $32½, a 35 strike price would be added. If it dropped to $22½, a 20 strike price would be added. The purpose of adding new strike price series is to have a strike price at a higher price than the stock so that cheap options will always be available.

Parenthetically, an option is on one hundred shares of stock in most cases. However, certain adjustments are sometimes required for a stock dividend, or a stock split. An adjustment is *never* made for a stock's ordinary dividend. Were a $60 stock to split two for one, the strike price of all the options would be cut in half when the split became effective and the number of shares of stock under option would increase from 100 shares to 200 shares. Thus a 60 strike price option on 100 shares would become a 30 strike price option on 200 shares. A 50 strike price option would become a 25 strike option on 200 shares. Lesser adjustments, but of the same kind, would be made for a 5 percent stock dividend.

In the OTC market, the cost of a new option is called "the premium," because the strike price is almost always the current market price of the stock under option. Thus, the premium is a pure cost charged for the use of the time specified by the option, since the option initially has no intrinsic value. However, with listed options, what one pays for an option may be all premium, or no premium at all, or anywhere in between. For example, all the XYZ 40 Call options in Table 1 have a strike price higher than that of the common. Consequently, the prices of these options are all pure time premium since Calls on a stock have no intrinsic value when the stock can be more cheaply bought in the open market. The price represents pure speculative hope that the stock will advance during the life of the Call. Such options are usually referred to as out-of-the-money options. Prices in Table 1 are quoted in points, i.e., dollars per share. Thus, the XYZ May 40 Call quoted at 1¼ is equivalent to a price of $125 per option since the option is on one hundred shares.

On the other hand, all of the XYZ 30 Calls have very little time premium. Reflect a minute. The owner of a Call acquires the right, in return for the money he pays, to buy the stock at the strike price of the option at any time during the duration of the option. Using the XYZ February 30 Call as an example, by paying 5⅝ points ($562.50) one could buy XYZ at 30 for a total of 35⅝ before commissions. However, the stock on the open market is 34¾. The difference between these two, ⅞ of a point, is time premium. The rest of the option price, 5⅝ less ⅞ or 4¾ points, represents *instrinsic* or real value. Such an option is termed as in-the-money.

The XYZ 35 Calls are called at-the-money options. The strike price of the options are very close to the current stock price. Yet, the price of the options reflects either all or nearly all time premium.

To understand the logic of Put options, you must simply reverse your thinking completely. The owner of a Put has acquired the right, in return for the money paid, to sell one hundred shares of stock (to put it) at the strike price of the option at any time during the duration of the option. Again referring to Table 1, all the 30 strike price Puts are out-of-the-money options. Clearly the right to sell XYZ at 30 when it can be sold in the open market at 34¾ has no intrinsic value other than the hope that the stock might decline below 30 before the option expires.

On the other hand, the XYZ 40 Puts are in-the-money options since the right to sell a stock at a price higher than the going market clearly has intrinsic value. The February 40 Put costs 5⅜ points. Selling stock at 40 and subtracting the cost of the Put results in an effective sale price of 40 less 5⅜ or 34⅝. Since XYZ can be sold in the marketplace at 34¾, the price of the Put

Table 2   Summary of Terminology XYZ @ 34¾

Strike Price		May Expiration		
		Calls	Puts	
40	(out-of-the-money)	1¼	5¾	(in-the-money)
35	(at-the-money)	3¼	2⅝	(at-the-money)
30	(in-the-money)	6¼	⅞	(out-of-the-money)

carries ⅛ of a point time premium. The rest of the price constitutes intrinsic value. In the prior example of the in-the-money February 30 Call, the time premium was ⅞ of a point. Our corresponding May in-the-money Put only carries ⅛ point premium. This discrepancy is neither random nor accidental. In-the-money Puts almost always have less time premium than their Call counterparts. In fact, all Put options are almost always less expensive than their mirror image Call counterparts. The reason for this, and its implications, will be discussed in a later section.

Winding up this segment on terminology, with the XYZ example the 35 strike Puts are the at-the-money options, just as are the 35 strike Calls. Were XYZ to either advance or decline a couple of dollars, no option, either Put or Call, would be an at-the-money option. The particular significance of at-the-money options will be seen when the leverage considerations of buying options is later discussed.

THE PRICE OF HOPE

The premium that one will pay for an option is a function of the estimated profit potential over the life of the option, factored by the amount of risk. The further the option is in-the-money, the greater is its intrinsic value. The greater the intrinsic value, the *greater the cost,* and consequently the *greater the risk* of loss. This is why the more expensive options with a common expiration date will have the lesser premium.

On the other side of the coin, all options are good for only a limited period of time. The longer the option has to run, the

Table 3   Percent Premium of XYZ Calls with Stock @ 34¾

Strike Price	Intrinsic Value	February			May			August		
		Price	Premium		Price	Premium		Price	Premium	
		($)	($)	(%)	($)	($)	(%)	($)	($)	(%)
40	0	⅜R	⅜	100	1¼	1¼	100	2⅛	2⅛	100
35	0	1⅞	1⅞	100	3¼	3¼	100	4⅜	4⅜	100
30	4¾	5⅝	⅞	16	6¼	1½	24	7⅛	7⅛	33

more time there is for the option to turn a profit. Tables 3 and 4 demonstrate that time is indeed money.

The amount of time premium increases for a given strike price with each successively longer expiration period. The 30 Calls, the 40 Puts, and the 35 Puts show this phenomenon clearly. As a corollary, the price of an option will decrease to its intrinsic value (as time passes). If the option is out-of-the-money and thereby has no intrinsic value, the price will drop to zero.

DEATH IN THE AFTERNOON

As a brief aside, option time is different from people time. Our lives are circumscribed by so many days, each one just twenty-four hours long. From birth to death we each walk with a steady measured step toward our fate. However, options do not age

Table 4   Percent Premium of XYZ Puts with Stock @ 34¾

Strike Price	Intrinsic Value	February			May			August		
		Price	Premium		Price	Premium		Price	Premium	
		($)	($)	(%)	($)	($)	(%)	($)	($)	(%)
40	5¼	5⅜	⅛	2	5¾	½	9	6¼	1	16
35	¼	1⅝	1⅜	85	2⅝	2⅜	90	3⅜	3⅛	92
30	0	¼	¼	100	⅞	⅞	100	1¼	1¼	100

Graph 1   Generalized option price versus time curve

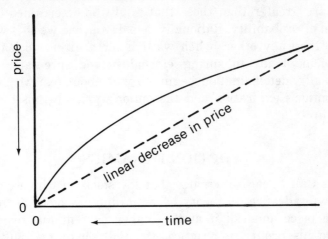

uniformly. They don't shed value proportionate with the passage of time.

This phenomenon particularly applies to at-the-money options, both Puts and Calls. The February 35 Call in Table 1 with two months left should be worth two-fifths of the May 25 Call with five months left, if prices decayed linearly. Yet, the real price is 1⅞, not the 1¼ that results from the above calculation. The February 35 Put should be priced at two-fifths the price of the May 35 Put, or 1, not the 1⅝ priced in the market. The same is true for the May 35 Puts and Calls when compared to the August Puts and Calls.

Investor expectations are influenced by a wide variety of factors: earnings per share, economic projections, political decisions, big labor negotiations, international situations, weather, and innumerable others. This complex skein of events must be weighed and evaluated. They are not amenable to any arithmetic niceties. Projecting the future is an art, not a science. Also, a large dose of hope is intimately involved in any forecasting effort.

Hope's most conspicuous attribute is tenacity, a willingness to struggle on in the face of insurmountable odds, and unwillingness to give up. Such stubbornness accounts for options prices that are greater than those that might be determined by some model of probability. Rationally, one day or one week is worth no more than any other, when waiting for a given stock to move. But hope tends to spring eternal in the speculator's heart. Normally, determination begins to wilt about five weeks before the option's expiration and the option's price begins to rapidly cave in.

OPTION DYNAMICS

The Call buyer anticipates that the stock on which he buys a Call will advance. In theory he would buy the stock at the lower strike price and sell it at the higher current market price to secure his profit. In practice, the Call buyer normally would realize his profit by selling his appreciated option in the exchange-traded secondary market. The commission for selling the option is considerably less than that involved in exercising the option on one hundred shares and, in turn, reselling this stock in the open market.

The Put buyer anticipates that the stock on which he buys a Put will decline. In theory, he would make his profit by buying the depreciated stock at its lower current market value and Putting (selling) it at the higher option strike price. Just as with Calls, it will usually be more practical to realize any profit by selling the Put in the secondary options market.

In summary: *The price of Calls increases in a rising market, while the price of Puts declines. In a falling market, the price of Calls will decline and the price of Puts advance.*

MOUNTAIN-MOVING LEVERAGE

While options can be used for purposes both conservative and speculative, by far the greatest number of option buyers are basically gamblers. As the old saying goes, "They pays their money and they takes their chances." Just as in Las Vegas, a definite sum of money is put up in the expectation of the possibility of a vastly greater return.

Unlike his Las Vegas brethren, however, the option buyer actually buys *control* over the capital he is betting on. In everyday terms, anyone who borrows money does the same thing. In the case of a borrower, the price paid for control is the interest charge.

In buying a mortgaged house, the home owner gets all the advantages of a house that was partially paid for with someone else's money. If the value of the house appreciates, the owner reaps the profit, not the lender. Unfortunately, such an advantage seldom accrues if one borrows money to buy an automobile. For better or worse, the idea of deriving all the benefits of money one doesn't have, but can borrow, is the mainspring of the whole economy of the United States. The buyer risks the money he lays out as a down payment. The lender takes a somewhat lesser risk in return for the charges he assesses.

Also unlike gamblers in Las Vegas, where the bet is placed in the face of certain mathematical odds that dictate the probable outcome, the option buyer is doing more than just playing the odds. He's playing his judgment and experience in the market. He is gambling that he can predict the outcome based on his interpretation of facts, actions and reactions, opinions, and all the myriad forces that interact in the marketplace. While this is gambling of a sort, it is a lot more sophisticated and complicated than pulling the arm on a slot machine.

Let's look at an example that will put these elements of leverage and risk in concrete terms. As I mentioned before, the stock known as XYZ in Table 1 is a very real security, disguised so that the reader might not be misled into concluding that the price relationships between the stock and its options are immutably cast in cement. Nonetheless, the security is quite real, actively traded, and somewhat more volatile than the market of stocks as a whole. During 1978, it swung from a low of 23⅛ to a high of 43¼. Over the five-year period from 1974 through 1978, the price had a high-low range of 43¼ to 7⅝. All in all, the stock is a remarkably appropriate candidate for options speculation.

With such a price history, it is hardly inconceivable that the stock, priced at 34¾ in the example, could advance or decline as much as ten points over an eight month period, depending upon the swirling forces that might impact the economy and the market.

Let us examine the various techniques by which one could turn a favorable move into profit. And the associated risks if one's mind's eye were astigmatic.

Control of the XYZ stock can be accomplished by any of three alternatives. The stock itself could be bought outright for cash, the stock could be bought on margin, or the same control could be bought using the August 35 Call. Each approach has entirely different risk/reward characteristics.

One hundred shares would cost $3,475 if fully paid for, and $1,738 if the purchase were fully margined at 50 percent, with the broker lending the investor the balance. The cost of buying the Call option would be $438. (In Table 1 the quoted price of the August 35 Call is 4⅜.) While options may be bought in either a cash or margin account, they are not marginable. They must always be fully paid for. In this example, I will ignore the commission costs because they have a relatively negligible impact. Such is not always the case.

About the only item in Table 5 that is not wholly self explanatory is the Call option price of $975 after XYZ advanced to 44¾. Recalling that the Call is the right to buy XYZ at 35, when XYZ is trading at 44¾, the option must be worth approximately its intrinsic value or the difference between the two prices, 44¾ less 35 or 9¾ points. I say approximately because there are two

**Table 5   Upside Leverage Using Margin and August 35 Call
(all figures in dollars unless otherwise noted)**

Buyer Type	Price @ 34¾			Price @ 44¾			Gain	Gain (%)
	Market Value	Debit Balance	Cash Equity	Market Value	Debit Balance	Cash Equity		
Cash	3,475	—	3,475	4,475	—	4,475	1,000	29
Margin	3,475	1,737	1,738	4,475	1,737	2,738	1,000	58
Call	438	—	438	975	—	975	537	123

reasons that such an in-the-money option might trade for some-what more or somewhat less than its intrinsic value. If XYZ had reached the higher price in the example in early August, the August 35 Call would only have a week or two left before expiration. With so little time left, the option might actually trade at a slight discount because of the lack of speculative interest in such a short-lived expensive option.

On the other hand, had XYZ made its advance by March or April, the August 35 Call would probably be trading for some-what more than its intrinsic value of 9¾ because of the amount of life left in the option.

Regardless of whether the Call option trades at a slight discount or a premium over its intrinsic value, the leverage of the Call over either a cash or margin purchase of the stock is quite pronounced. A 29 percent move in the stock results in a 123 percent profit using the Call.

If the profit leverage is so superb, let's look at the risk side of the situation. What if our judgment of XYZ is wrong. Earnings didn't improve as expected, the new product introduction was a failure, the treasurer embezzled all the corporate cash, or the anticipated bull market turned out to be a bear trap. What if the ten point advance became a ten point decline.

High leverage is usually accompanied by high risk. Such is certainly the case with commodity futures. When option risk is compared with common stock risk, option risk is considerably less. Options are to the underlying stocks as playful waves are to the ocean depths. As can be seen in Table 6, when stock control is acquired by ownership of the security the *dollar* risks can be much larger than those realized with an expiring option. Cer-

Table 6   Downward Leverage Using Margin and August 35 Call (all figures in dollars unless otherwise noted)

Buyer Type	Price @ 34¾			Price @ 24¾			Loss	Loss (%)
	Market Value	Debit Balance	Cash Equity	Market Value	Debit Balance	Cash Equity		
Cash	3,475	—	3,475	2,475	—	2,475	1,000	29
Margin	3,475	1,737	1,738	2,475	1,737	738	1,000	58
Call	438	—	438	0	—	0	438	100

Graph 2   Profits and losses at different XYZ prices

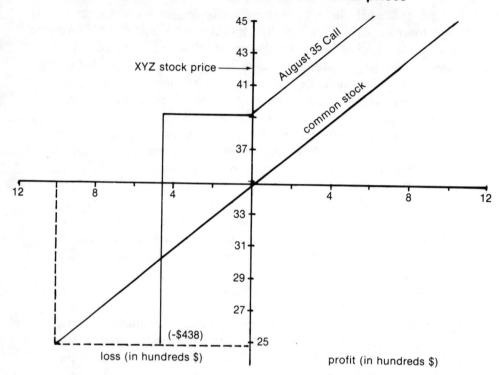

loss (in hundreds $)   profit (in hundreds $)

tainly the August 35 Call would expire with XYZ at 24¾. While the *percentage* loss is less for the stockholder, that's only because he had a much larger investment. It's not because his was a favored investment *under the circumstances*.

Recapitulating, options have advantages as leverage for a large, favorable price movement of the underlying stock combined with limited risk if the subsequent movement is largely unfavorable. The preceding analysis could just as well apply to Put options. In that case, the anticipated move would have been sharply down instead of up.

THE HOOK

High leverage, limited risk. What else could a speculator ask for? Has the millenium dawned?

Graph 3 Percent profits and losses at different XYZ prices

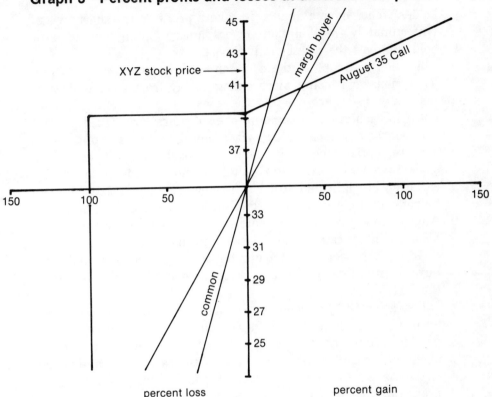

The answer is, of course, Yes and No. Options are a very useful tool. But there is a *hook*.

Graphs 2 and 3 depict the risk/reward outcomes at a whole range of common stock prices, and both clearly demonstrate the principal drawback of options. The Call option is a dead loss, a wipe out, if XYZ doesn't advance beyond 35, the strike price of the option, before it expires the third week in August. In fact, if XYZ just manages to reach 39⅜ on the above date, the Call buyer will simply break even. This price is derived from the strike price of 35 plus the Call price of 4⅜. With the listed options secondary market, were XYZ to advance sharply before the expiration and then fall back below 35, the Call option holder would have a chance to take a profit on the short swing. Unfortunately, most option buyers ignore timing and tend to hold well past their best profit opportunity.

As seen in Graph 2, the common stock immediately makes or loses money with any price change away from 34¾. It doesn't make any difference whether the stock was bought on margin or not if in each case the same number of shares are owned. As the common advances from 34¾, it promptly accrues profit. However, the option frequently has to earn back part of its cost via a stock advance before it starts making money. The option buyer can even be right and still lose money. The key is that he must be right in a big way, not a small one. At a stock price of $37 in August, the option buyer would be able to salvage two points of his 4⅜-point investment to at least limit his loss.

Graph 3 reflects the margin buyer's, cash buyer's, and Call buyer's situation by plotting percentage profit and loss versus the XYZ price.

Just as in the previous graph, the Call buyer is under water until XYZ hits 39⅜. At this same point the cash buyer has a 13 percent profit and the margin buyer a 27 percent profit. At about 40 the Call buyer goes ahead of the cash buyer and ahead of the margin buyer at 41. After 41, the Call buyer's percentage profit rapidly outstrips that of the stock owners.

On the downside, the Call holder has a 100 percent loss without the stock even dropping. As XYZ declines, the margin buyer's loss accelerates relative to the cash buyer's for every point drop of the common.

Above all, these illustrations hammer away at the point that options are only attractive on highly volatile stocks. Small price movements are just as deadly as contrary price movements to the option buyer. It takes big swings in prices for the option holder to make a good profit.

It should be added that Graph 3 clearly illustrates that owning stocks on margin is a *highly* risky affair. Margined stocks are most perilous in a falling market and don't profit as well in a *rapidly* rising market, compared to Calls.

YOU CAN'T FLOAT WEARING A LEAD VEST

The common thread that runs through the whole of the prior section is *control*. A cash buyer is compared to a margin buyer and then again to an option holder. The common denominator in all cases is the same number of shares. For simplicity, I used 100 shares. The generalizations regarding relative leverage and risk are sound as long as each alternative is compared on an equal footing. To equate one hundred shares bought outright with two hundred shares bought on margin and further again with buying ten options on the same stock would be *outrageous*. The only common denominator is the approximate amount of cash required. However, both the possible rewards along with the attendant risks escalate dramatically. Buying the common stock of even the most flamboyant company is considerably more conservative than using the same money to buy options. While common stock has no redemption price and date like a bond, it might pay a dividend and very seldom expires except under the most dire financial circumstances. Options generate no return (other than possible appreciation) and they die as surely as the spring flowers. With the exception of a few legitimate hedge configurations, buying options varies from mildy speculative to grossly speculative. This degree is determined by the financial and emotional makeup of each individual investor.

Successful options trading requires the utmost restraint because of the temptation to eat all the goodies on the table. A man who can afford to buy 100 shares of Dupont at a pre-split price of 140 often thinks nothing of buying options on 1,000 shares. If this particular trader makes a profit, he is liable to move up to ten options on IBM at a pre-split price of 310. And he will trade until his capital, profits, and all are gone. There are *old* traders, there are *bold* traders—but there are no *old, bold* traders.

A wise option trader pays attention to the same rules as a prudent portfolio manager:

Avoid overconcentration in any one situation.

Recognize the value of diversification of strategies, types of
   options, and underlying stocks.
Faithfully adhere to your investment objectives.
Take losses quickly and profits slowly.
Use every tool available to analyze the most probable specula-
   tions.
Always eschew tips and gossip.
Never fight the market regardless of your convictions.

These are the precepts of the wise trader. They are much
easier to enumerate than follow. It is reported that Alfred Lord
Keynes, the renowned economist, made a fortune without leaving
the comfort of his bed. He supposedly read voraciously and
associated with only the most influential people in London. I
suggest that if the reader doesn't have a stock or two wired, he
had better get out of bed and off to his broker's library.

VOLATILITY—FASTER THAN A SPEEDING BULLET

Buyers of Puts and Calls abhor a dull market. Small erratic
price changes are irritating and unprofitable. The clock ticks,
time passes, seemingly attractive investments evaporate. Successful speculating with options requires volatility. Stock prices
must move up briskly for the Call buyer and plummet for the
Put buyer. Happiness is a yo-yo.

As the graph vividly demonstrates, there has been enough
price movement to gratify the most jaded options trader. The
market has been booming and busting with almost methodical
regularity since 1966. Average common stock prices have
doubled and then been halved in reaction. Individual issues have
tripled during the upswing and then plunged to catastrophic
lows when stocks were put under the hammer. Undoubtedly,
this unprecedented violence has provided considerable impetus
to the explosive growth of the listed options industry.

The stock market is a mirror, reflecting the nation's prospects
with prices. The market chaos of the last thirteen years portrays
uncertainty propelled by powerful crosscurrents. Of historical

Graph 4 Dow Jones Industrial Average history from 1926 to 1979

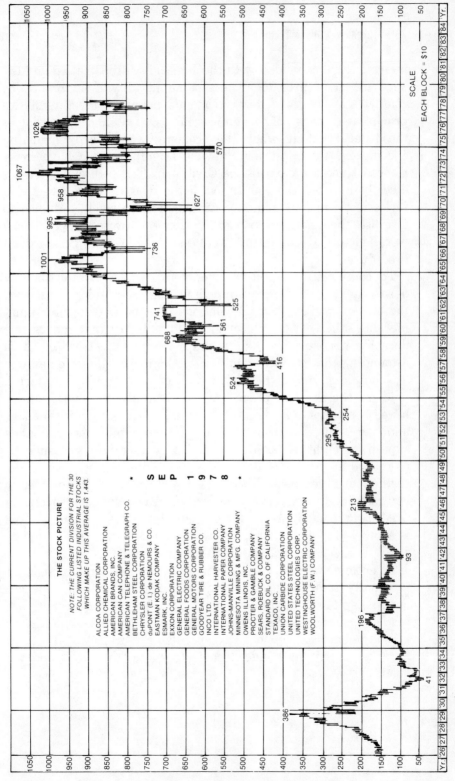

THE STOCK PICTURE

NOTE: THE CURRENT DIVISION FOR THE 30
FOLLOWING LISTED INDUSTRIAL STOCKS
WHICH MAKE UP THIS AVERAGE IS 1.443.

ALCOA CORPORATION
ALLIED CHEMICAL CORPORATION
AMERICAN BRANDS, INC.
AMERICAN CAN COMPANY
AMERICAN TELEPHONE & TELEGRAPH CO.   *
BETHLEHAM STEEL CORPORATION
CHRYSLER CORPORATION   S
duPONT (E. I.) de NEMOURS & CO.   E
EASTMAN KODAK COMPANY   P
ESMARK, INC.
EXXON CORPORATION
GENERAL ELECTRIC COMPANY
GENERAL FOODS CORPORATION   1
GENERAL MOTORS CORPORATION   9
GOODYEAR TIRE & RUBBER CO.   7
INCO LTD.   8
INTERNATIONAL HARVESTER CO.
INTERNATIONAL PAPER COMPANY
JOHNS-MANVILLE CORPORATION
MINNESOTA MINING & MFG. COMPANY   *
OWENS ILLINOIS, INC.
PROCTER & GAMBLE COMPANY
SEARS, ROEBUCK & COMPANY
STANDARD OIL CO. OF CALIFORNIA
TEXACO, INC.
UNION CARBIDE CORPORATION
UNITED STATES STEEL CORPORATION
UNITED TECHNOLOGIES CORP.
WESTINGHOUSE ELECTRIC CORPORATION
WOOLWORTH (F. W.) COMPANY

SCALE

EACH BLOCK = $10

interest, 1966 coincided with the Johnson administration and the Vietnam adventure. Regardless of the morality of our role in the conflict, clearly the federal economic policy in the late sixties precipitated "times of economic troubles." The huge expansion of the federal deficit when the economy was already churning encouraged the most brutal wave of inflation we have experienced since the close of the Civil War. The politicians, having directly infected the country with the disease, then invented a series of pernicious symptomatic cures purposively designed to disguise their own responsibility for the cause. If politicians were doctors, bloodletting would still be a common medical procedure.

To compound the federal ineptness, we have unfortunately been visited with a host of uninvited disasters: Middle East war, the oil embargo, OPEC, revolutions in Africa, Iran, plus innumerable other crises in morality and industry that makes this decade's history play like a soap opera. In retrospect, it is astounding that we have muddled through as well as we have.

Nonethless, this hyperactive market has provided a fertile field for the skillful options trader. Certainly, the opportunities have been there. All the speculator has to do is zig with the zigs and zag with the zags. Of course, such nimbleness demands superb foresight. After all, predicting is essentially guessing the unknowable. And the unknowable is increasingly obscure the farther one reaches. Witness a market that has completely reversed its direction every one or two years. But then success in predicting usually results from predicting quite frequently. This is another way of saying that a wise man keeps his commitments small, is energetic, and doesn't let his wits dull.

As enticing as this volatile market environment might seem, it is equally treacherous. Zigging on a zag phase can wipe out option capital virtually overnight. The stuff that dreams are made of can easily become a nightmare. One lapse, one serious misjudgment can demolish a speculator's firepower. In these days, the Lord shall indeed come to judge "the quick and the dead."

The implications of these hazards and opportunities should be understood:

(1) There are many investors and even some speculators who should never trade options, regardless of the strategy employed, because of limited financial circumstances, or unsuitable investment objectives.

(2) Only a complete fool would ever commit more than *15 percent* of his total discretionary investment capital to the purchase of options. Options are where the action is. If the speculator is adept, such a portion will provide ample rewards. If he flops, the bulk of his capital is still intact. *Overinvesting is undoubtedly the most grievous sin committed by amateurs and professionals alike.*

(3) Speaking of amateurs and professionals, the difference between the two is knowledge. There is no need to trade like an amateur, make foolish mistakes or needlessly lose money in a treacherous market when a little study and effort can increase your probabilities for profit.

THEORETICAL VALUE

Mathematicians savor fame as much as the next man. While their machinations tend to be recondite and often not of any obvious benefit other than as raw material for succeeding mathematicians, they can smell out opportunity like a pig hunting truffles. Coincidently with the opening of the CBOE, Drs. Fisher Black of the University of Chicago and Myron Scholes of M.I.T. published a paper in the *Journal of Political Economy* entitled "The Pricing of Options and Corporate Liabilities." As prudent academicians wisely hedging against impecunious glory, it was noted that the work was supported in part by the Ford Foundation.

Their initial work immediately generated considerable interest in the theoretical valuation or "normal" value of an option. Purportedly, if the real option was actually trading in the marketplace cheaper than its theoretical value, the option was *undervalued.* If trading at a higher price, it was *overvalued.* The semantic inference was obvious: the adroit speculator should only buy undervalued options and sell overvalued options. Liberated from the pitfalls of messy human judgment, the strategy had the earmarks of scientific certainty. If such an innovation worked in practice, clearly the precarious art of investing would be revolutionized—*if it worked.*

Mathematical logic requires that the underlying premise from which all the numeric manipulations will flow must first be stated. If the foundation is a wee bit rickety, the final structure is suspect regardless of the strengths of the proofs. I will quote the first two sentences of their presupposition:

> If options are correctly priced in the market, it should not be possible to make sure profits by creating portfolios of long and short positions in options and their underlying stocks. Using this principle, a theoretical valuation formula for options is derived.

Mathematics, like religion, expounds certain universal truths. In my mind, the above statement recites the obvious. If some mythical, universal investor held all the stock and all the options in the whole market, his performance could be no better than that of the whole market. This is the *Random Walk Theory* dressed up in a suit of clothes with options pockets. The beauty of the theory is that it can be statistically proven. Such concrete evidence really excites academe.

But what about you and me who are destined to plug along with the drudgery of our individual reality? Does the theory, when particularized, guarantee that since we can't do any better, we obviously can't do any worse? Hardly. Your experience and mine convinces us both that no universal or average generalization describes our own unique circumstances. The Black-Scholes premise applies to *everyone*, but *not* to *one*. I would suggest that a principle that is useless to individuals is equally useless when applied in the aggregate.

Regardless of my scepticism of erudite pomposity, of the possible irrelevancy of some mechanical equation, we should briefly examine the theoretical valuation formula if for no other reason than its popular currency.

$$w(x, t) \;=\; xN(d_1) \;-\; ce^{r(t-t^*)} N(d_2)$$

$$\text{where } d_1 \;=\; \frac{\ln\frac{x}{c} \;+\; (r \;+\; \tfrac{1}{2}v^2)(t^*-t)}{v\ \sqrt{t^*-t}}$$

$$\text{and } d_2 \;=\; \frac{\ln\frac{x}{c} \;+\; (r \;-\; \tfrac{1}{2}v^2)(t^*-t)}{v\ \sqrt{t^*-t}}$$

At the time t, when the stock price is x, the value of the option is w (x,t). The exercise price is c, t* is the time at which the option expires, r is the interest rate, ln is the natural logarithm, v^2 is the measure of the stock's volatility, and N(d) is the cummulative normal density function.

I presume you are suitably impressed—or awestruck. Years ago when I lingered in the halls of learning, I successfully completed a course in differential calculus and I still carry a fond tinge of nostalgia for the certainty and security of a formula. Such a construction superficially broaches no argument and stands impregnably on its own merits.

But does it really represent some useful reality? Are all the hundreds and thousands of computer hours that are spent by the brokerage houses and advisory services in calculating theoretical option values profitably spent? You can probably anticipate my answer. NO! The reason is simple. The formula is an elaborate disguise for nothing more than sophisticated guesswork.

All the components of the equation are easily measured, i.e., time, price, prevailing interest rates. All *except one*, v^2, the measure of the stock's *volatility*. There are as many measures as there are people measuring. While there is a general agreement that volatility reflects the "gooseyness" of a stock's price, there is virtually no consensus of how it should be calculated. Is last month's price action more important than last year's? Is yesterday's more important than last month's? And how should they be weighted? I know one wizard who weighted yesterday 90 percent, and the previous two years 10 percent. If all men carry a different key that opens the same lock, there's nothing behind the door worth stealing.

Finally, I believe there is a fatal philosophical error in presuming that any calculated index of historic volatility has reliable short-term predictive validity. Certainly anyone who had developed a magic touchstone that could foresee the price range of IBM for the coming year, for instance, would never merchandise their secret. They'd be at their own brokers or at the race track, or Las Vegas, or Atlantic City cleaning up millions with their "system." Besides, the successful prediction of volatility is only slightly related to trading profits. The trend, either up or down, is where the money is made. An undervalued Call on IBM, even were the analyst prescient in his measurement of future volatility, is a terrible investment if IBM is not already in, or does not quickly move into, an uptrend.

All of which brings me to describe an interesting anomaly. Several of the most skillful option traders I know *only buy overvalued* options. And their logic is as follows: An option trading at "normal" value reflects an orderly market climate in which virtually all the known and anticipated information about the stock has already been factored into the stock's price. However, aggressive option buying interest, the kind that drives options prices to overvalued levels, oftentimes precedes very favorable news. Overvalued options usually identify underlying stocks already in a strong trend or ones on the verge of a breakout into vigorous trading activity. In either case, the probabilities of option profits are substantially higher than with dull, lackluster, thoroughly discounted stocks.

Having attempted to discredit the general usefulness of theoretical option valuation, I must now admit that there is one instance in which the computer-spawned tool can be valuable. The fallacy of "normal" option valuation hinges on the volatility calculation, since each technician's guess is no better than yours or mine. However, when the "normal" value of different options on the *same* underlying stock are compared, the effect of stock volatility is the same for each option. Thus, an investor might be able to identify the most favorable option on the stock, assuming he was already favorably disposed toward the stock for considerations other than the calculated volatility. Additionally, comparing the various options sometimes leads to attractive option spreading opportunities. Most of the time, only professionals can really capitalize on such situations because their trade costs are rather modest. However, every once in a while the disparity between two options will be large enough to be profitable for a retail investor. The most commonly used technique to exploit such disparities would be the ratio spread in one variation or another. This type of spreading activity will be covered in a later section.

4

The Bull Market

There are all kinds of bull markets. Some are as big as a house, sweeping all stock prices upward in the flush of ebullient enthusiasm. Others are small, sometimes only centering on one stock or maybe a group of stocks. In either event, the detection of the impending move requires considerable analysis and a large measure of intuition to help sort out the relevant from the irrelevant. A bell doesn't ring when the starting gates burst open.

BUYING CALLS

Historical data indicates that buyers of options very rarely make money. As Max G. Ansbacher stated in his book entitled *The New Options Market*, only 40 percent of options purchased are ever exercised and it is estimated that only 50 percent of those exercised are ever done so at a profit. On this basis, only one out of five Calls is profitable. Frankly, from my own personal experience, the probabilities are nowhere as sanguine. I have seen money lost, sometimes a trader's total capital, because of carelessness and impulsiveness. However, if one insists on speculating, I can offer guidelines for the decision making process. Such guidelines involve assessing the most attractive stock candidates and a determination of the most appropriate option as regards upside potential, leverage, and risk.

Certainly, the primary criterion in buying a Call is the proper selection of the underlying stock. Once convinced for whatever reason that a security is going to increase in value, the speculator should make an options analysis. If the option buyer knew with absolute certainty that XYZ would make a dramatic move in thirty days, he would buy the cheapest February option to get the maximum leverage on his investment. On the other hand, if he felt the stock might languish for thirty days before moving upward, he would ignore the February and only consider a May or August option. The point is that the buyer never *knows* either the timing or extent of the move beforehand. Rather, he is faced with a spectrum of probabilities. As opposed to an outright shot in the dark, the thoughtful speculator should consider the following approach to *conservative speculation:* A speculator should *never* buy an option with the idea of making a *small profit.* After all, if he is wrong, he will lose his whole investment. It is my belief that he should, at the very least, look for a situation in which he can double his money. This concept gives rise to the *double-your-money* analysis.

Table 7 was prepared by simply doubling the price of each option in Table 1 and then adding the amount to the strike price of the option involved. This generates the price to which the common stock must rise before expiration for the option to be worth twice as much as it cost. Doubling the February 35 at $1\frac{7}{8}$ yields $3\frac{3}{4}$. Adding the $3\frac{3}{4}$ to the 35 strike price means that the stock must advance to $38\frac{3}{4}$ for the February 35 to double in price. The percent move from the current price of $34\frac{3}{4}$ is then calculated. This same procedure is followed for each option.

Table 7   Percent move of XYZ to Double Call Option Price (Stock @ 34¾)

	February (2 months left)			May (5 months left)		
Strike Price	Common Price to Double Option	Option Price	Percent Common Change	Common Price to Double Option	Option Price	Percent Common Change
40	40¾	¾	17.3	42½	2½	22.3
35	38¾	3¾	11.5	41½	6½	19.4
30	41¼	11¼	18.7	42½	12½	22.3

August (8 months left)		
Common Price to Double Option	Option Price	Percent Common Change
44¼	4½	27.3
43¾	8¾	25.9
44¼	14¼	27.3

Examination of Table 7 reveals several worthwhile generalizations:

(1) the *longer* options always *require* a *greater* percentage *move* in the common to be as profitable *as* the *nearby*. Of course, there is correspondingly more time for the move to take place.

(2) The *in-the-money options require* a *greater move* in the common *than those* options whose *strike price is closer* to the current stock price. This is because they initially cost more.

(3) The *most attractive* option to buy will *always* be the *one* whose *strike price* is just a *little* bit *above* or a little bit *below* the *current stock* price. In the present example, the February 35 is the most attractive February option because the stock must advance the least for the option to double. Only the individual speculator can judge whether he thinks it more likely that XYZ will advance 11.5 percent in sixty days or 19.4 percent in five months for the May 35 Call to achieve the same level of profitability.

This last point brings up another dimension: the element of

Table 8   Percent/Month Move of XYZ to Double Call Option Price

Strike Price	February (2 months left)		May (5 months left)		August (8 months left)	
	Percent Common	% per Month	Percent Common	% per Month	Percent Common	% per Month
40	17.3	8.6	22.3	4.5	27.3	3.4
35	11.5	5.7	19.4	3.9	25.9	3.2
30	18.7	9.3	22.3	4.5	27.3	3.4

time. The probability that an option price will double in two months is patently much less than the probability that it will double in five months, and still less again than its chance of doubling in eight months.

The more time, the greater the likelihood that the expected event will occur. Given enough time, even the end of the world will assuredly come. Table 8 reflects the impact of this increased probability over time by dividing the "percent move to double option price" figure in Table 7 by the remaining months of option life.

Viewed in this perspective, the longer options require a much lower percent move *per month* for the common stock to turn a handsome 100 percent profit from the option. If price advances followed steady upward trends, this type of presentation would be most representative. Since price moves frequently occur rather dramatically and then settle down to a period of relative stability, the percent move per month for the common stock is not wholly accurate. Nonetheless, this approach is one way to acknowledge the probabilistic advantage of having more time. As in Table 7, which was adjusted for the time factor, the option with the strike price closest to the stock price at the time the option is bought is still the most attractive option to buy from the standpoint of leverage.

Of course, time is money, particularly with options. The farther out the option, the higher the premium. It is interesting to note, however, that the more time one buys, the less it costs per unit. It's like a volume discount. The premium cost per month for five months is always much less than the cost per month for the first two months.

CAVEAT

I have repeatedly commented on the financial risks in buying wasting option assets. Earlier in the book, I rang the tocsin on the dangers of overinvesting in options. Now I would like to show you a magical piece of prestidigitation whereby a combination of negatives become positive.

Without waxing philosophic, risk is an undeniable aspect of investment. It cannot be completely eliminated, only mollified, adjusted, balanced. A portfolio of government securities has an extremely low, but nonetheless finite, level of risk. A portfolio made up only of options has an extremely high level of risk associated with it. By combining these juxtaposed extremes in various degrees, a portfolio can be constructed with total risk characteristics equivalent to any desired level of exposure.

As an example, let us theorize a completely risk-averse portfolio. By risk averse, I mean that at the end of any one year period every single dollar of capital must be intact. Cash in a safety deposit box would meet the criteria. Risk averse, yes—but profit averse as well. A portfolio design with the same risk restraints, but with a positive profit potential would incorporate treasury bills and options with heavy emphasis on the bills. An appropriate balance for a $100,000 model would consist of one $100,000 treasury bill with the remainder used to *buy* options on some more or less uniform basis over the course of the year. Treasury bills are bought at a discount and redeemed at face value. Thus, a one year 8 percent bill would cost a little more than $92,000. $100,000 would be due the investor at the end of the one year. The investor is assured of ending the year with the same number of dollars he started with. The uninvested cash, a little less than $8,000, would be used to buy either Calls or Puts or a combination of both depending upon market outlook. If all the options expire, the investor is still whole. If he is somewhat successful in his options selection, he could turn in an excellent overall portfolio performance without being exposed to the higher risk level associated with an exclusively common stock portfolio.

This approach demonstrates that preconceptions in investments are no more foolish than prejudgments are in life itself. Pure speculation is as rare as unadulterated evil. Options are not necessarily speculative or conservative. It all depends on *how they're used.*

The drawbacks of this relatively conservative deployment of options are twofold: one real, one psychological. In an inflationary age, simply holding the same number of dollars over any period of time *constitutes a real loss* of capital. Capital's value hinges on purchasing power, not in mere numbers, and as purchasing power erodes, so does capital. The second drawback stems from the very human propensity to become easily discouraged. Given two years of back to back failure in the options market, as an instance, there are few investors who would persevere on such a hopeless task, regardless of the intellectual nicety.

BULL SPREADING WITH CALLS

The *bull spread* is an alternative to the outright purchase of an option. This tactical variation, wherein both an option purchase and option sale are combined like a marriage, has both advantages and disadvantages. The bull spread with Calls involves buying the lower strike price Call and selling a higher strike price Call with the same expiration. In the XYZ example, buying a February 35 and selling a February 40 Call, or buying a May 35 and selling a May 40 Call are both bull spreads. In each case, the Call bought is near-the-money and the Call sold is out-of-the-money. The reason for this configuration will become apparent.

The purpose of selling the higher strike Call, even though the spreader fully expects the stock and related options to advance,

Table 9   Bull spreading with XYZ Calls (XYZ @ 34¾)

Strike Price	February (2 months)	May (5 months)
40	Sell ⅜ R	Sell 1¼
35	Buy 1⅞	Buy 3¼
30	5⅝	6¼

is to offset part of his risk. The financial risk faced by a buyer is that his option will expire worthless. Therefore, his total risk is the price of the option bought. If he can somehow buy a Call at a discounted price, he has reduced his risk. Bull spreading is the technique for doing this. The sale price of the Call sold reduces the amount of money required to buy the near-the-money Call.

Referring to Table 9, 1⅞ or $187.50 is required to buy one February 35 outright. By selling one February 40 for ⅜ or $37.50, this initial cost can be reduced to $150 or 1½ points. If XYZ common advances to 40 just before the expiration of the Calls, the February 40 sold short at ⅜ will expire with no value and the February 35 Call will have moved up from 1⅞ to 5. The bull spreader will have realized a profit of $37.50 from his short sale and a long side profit of 5 less 1⅞ paid or 3⅛ points which equals $312.50. The total profit would be $37.50 plus $312.50 or $350. The impact of commissions has been excluded for simplicity, but will be dealt with shortly.

By the way, you've probably noticed the letter R next to the price of the February 40 Call. The letter connotes that the option is *restricted*. No opening position to either buy or sell any option may be executed if the option closed the previous day at *less than ½ and* the strike price of the option is *more than 5 points* away from the previous close of the underlying stock. Fortunately, there is an exception. An opening position may be taken in a restricted option *if* that particular trade is part of a spread order. This simply means that one can't buy the February 35s one day and sell the February 40s the next. The two trades must be entered on the same day and be conditional upon one another. In other words, the order must be a legitimate spread order.

This exception was begrudgingly granted by the Securities and Exchange Commission, the very same body which in their overwhelming wisdom had promulgated that buying what it termed was a restricted option was egregiously speculative and therefore prohibited. Given full rein, the government will always plow everyone else's field.

Now, back to the mainstream issue. By entering into a bull spread, the spreader did indeed *reduce his risk* by $37.50 per spread. However, he paid a price. He *limited his profit*. If he was long on the February 35 by itself, his potential profit is virtually unlimited, assuming the stock took off like a rocket. In a bull spread, he can never make more than $350 per spread, because once the stock passes $40, every dollar made on the long side is eaten up by a corresponding loss on the short side. The *maximum profit* that can ever be realized in a bull spread is the *cost of the spread subtracted from* the *difference in strike prices* of the two options.

Performing this arithmetic operation on the February 30–February 35 combination shows why this spread can't be considered a useful bull spread. If one bought the February 30 Call for 5⅝ and sold the February 35 Call for 1⅞, the cost of this spread would be 3¾ points or $375. Yet, the maximum possible profit is the difference in strike prices (35 minus 30 equals 5) less the cost of the spread (3¾) or 1¼ points. Risking $375 with the hope of only making $125 borders on lunacy.

To summarize, the bull spreader reduces his risk at the expense of limiting his profit potential. In addition, he increases his commission cost since he is positioning two contracts instead of just one. In some instances, this commission cost can eat up a large portion of the profit. To be specific, if a spreader had bought five of the February 35–February 40 bull spreads for 1½ points, his cost would be five times $150 or $750 *plus* approximately $100 in commissions. Under the *best* of circumstances, assuming the February 40s expired and he sold his February 35s for 5 points, he would be staring down the barrel of another $85 in commissions. Thus, the realistic *minimum* commission cost could easily run to $185 to both establish and unwind the spread. Considering *total* costs, the real costs of the spread would actually be approximately $750 *plus* another $185 in commissions for a total of $935. As I've already pointed out, the maximum profit is 5 points, less the cost of the spread. For a five lot spread, that's $2,500 less the real cost of $935 or $1,565. Dividing the maximum real profit of $1,565 by the real cost of $935 results in a reward/risk ratio of 1.7. If this same computation is made before commissions, the reward/risk ratio is 3½ points divided by 1½, or 2.3. Obviously, commission costs can have a substantial impact upon the attractiveness of a particular spread strategy and should *never* be ignored.

Nonetheless, bull spreading with Calls is a useful tool for conservative speculating, because it reduces the risk and thereby increases the possibility of making *some* profit. Again referring to the XYZ example, the purchase of the February 35 Call at 1⅞ was an attractive buy because the stock had only to advance 11.5 percent for the option buyer to double his money. Were the buyer to have bull spread this same option by selling the February 40 against the February 35 for a cost of 1½ points, the stock would have to advance to no higher than 38 (two times 1½ plus 35) from 34¾ to double the value of the spread at expiration. This represents a somewhat more modest increase in the stock price of 9.3 percent. While more appealing from the probability standpoint than the straight purchase of the February 35 Call alone, it is still not a gift. The common still has to go up in the next sixty days to make any money at all. If XYZ doesn't move at all, the whole investment is down the drain.

You might have noticed that although Table 9 delineated both the February and May spreads, all my attention was directed toward the February spread. That's because the May spread is *nowhere near as attractive*. Superficially, the difference doesn't seem too great, but after commissions the relative attractiveness of the nearer February spread becomes quite apparent.

Buying the May 35 Call would cost 3¼ points, and selling the May 40 Call would reduce the cost by 1¼ points, leaving a net spread cost of 2 points. The maximum possible profit, just as with the February spread, is the difference in strike prices less the cost (5 less 2 points) or 3 points. Risking 2 points to make 3 isn't earth shattering odds, but all in all might still be attractive. *Until commissions costs are figured in.*

If five spreads were bought at 2 points or $200 each, the gross cost would be $1,000. However, both options are more expensive than their February counterparts. Consequently, the commission costs would rise at least to $130 to put on the spread. The minimum commissions to unwind the spread would still be about $85. The real cost of the spread would thus be approximately $1,215. Just as before, the maximum profit of five spreads would be $2,500 less the total cost of $1,215 or $1,285. The reward/risk ratio for the May spread is $1,285 divided by $1,215, or 1.1. To put this figure in perspective, it represents a probability only slightly better *than tossing a coin.* If any lesser number bull spreads than five were bought, the odds would become *progressively worse* because the impact of commissions is proportionately greater.

As a general observation, spreading is inherently more costly than the outright purchase of options. As far as bull spreads are concerned, the *nearer term spreads are almost always more attractive* than the most distant. They cost less in absolute terms and have more appealing reward/risk characteristics.

A Call bull spread, just like the outright long option position, has a 100 percent margin requirement. Unlike an outright option position which can be held in either the cash or the margin account, all spreads must be placed in the margin account. The spreader must fully pay for the cost of the long position after it is reduced by the proceeds received from the sale of the option sold. In addition, all brokers require a minimum equity in a spreading account, usually $2,000. This amount is required as a safeguard should the client either intentionally, or accidentally, close out only the long side while attempting to liquidate the spread, thereby exposing the account to the much higher risks and margin requirements of a naked short option.

BULL SPREADING WITH PUTS

As I've already mentioned, Calls and Puts are mirror images of one another. Consequently, a bull spread can be assembled with Puts as well as with Calls. As you might expect, the mechanics operate quite differently.

The above spread exhibit demonstrates the *only* instance in which a Put and a Call configuration is the same. *A bull spread with either type of option is always made up by the purchase of the lower exercise price option (usually at-the-money) and the sale of the higher.*

The logic of the Call bull spread hinges on the increase in the value of the long option component of the spread. As you might expect, a Put bull spread profits from a *decrease* in value of the short option component of the spread. Concentrating on the February Put bull spread for the same reasons that the February Call bull spread was studied, you will notice that the lower strike price option (February 35 Put at 1⅝) which is purchased is considerably less expensive than the higher strike Put (February 40 at 5⅜) which is sold. Instead of spending money to buy the spread as with its Call counterpart, cash in the amount of (5⅜ minus 1⅝) 3¾ points, or $375 per spread, actually flows into the account. And *this* $375 *credit represents the maximum possible profit.*

If you recall the dynamics of Puts, their value *drops* as the underlying stock *advances.* If XYZ reached 40 by the end of the third week in February, *both* the 35 strike and 40 strike price options will expire. Were that to happen, the spreader would be

Table 10   Bull Spreading with XYZ Puts (XYZ @ 34¾)

Strike Price	February (2 months)	May (5 months)
40	Sell 5⅜	Sell 5¾
35	Buy 1⅝	Buy 2⅝
30	¼	⅞

secure with his full $375 profit. The spreader has spent part of the proceeds from the *sale* of the February 40 Put to *buy* the February 35 Put as an *insurance policy*. Were the stock to fall back to 30 and the February 40 Put be exercised to the spreader, he would have to pay $40 per share for the one hundred shares underlying each Put option. However, he could then in turn exercise his February 35 Put and thereby receive at least $35 per share. His total risk were the above to happen would be the $5 per share loss on the hundred shares *less* the $375 he received when he sold the spread or $125 per spread. Commissions have been omitted so as not to confuse explanation of the principle.

The *margin requirement* for a Put bull spread is the difference of the strike prices of the options bought and sold. Of course, the $375 received when the spread was sold can be applied to the requirement. This, the net *cash requirement* is only $125. This requirement can be met with either cash or other unencumbered equity in the account.

On the surface, it would seem that the Put bull spread might be superior to the Call bull spread under the same circumstances. After all, the cost using Calls were $150 per spread, while the cash requirement for the Put variety was $125. The reward/ risk parameter seems to favor the use of the Put spread.

Granting that there is some dollar advantage to using Puts, there are two much larger disadvantages. Firstly, the *Put market* has *less liquidity* than the Call market. The investing public perennially has a more positive attitude toward the market and Puts just do not attract as much interest as Calls. The consequence is that the number of Puts that can be either bought or sold at a given price is usually less than with Calls. Also, the difference between the bid and asking price is frequently larger than with Calls. And, of course, there are presently many fewer Put stocks available than there are Call stocks. While the Put market might ultimately expand to all those securities on which there are Calls, I doubt that the liquidity factor will ever be comparable to that of Calls.

Secondly, Put bull spreads have a *tendency to prematurely self destruct.* The ticking bomb is the in-the-money Put that is sold. You will notice in Table 10 that the February 40 Put has an intrinsic value of 5¼ points. Yet, the price of the option is only 5⅜. There's a mere ⅛ point time premium with two months left to run! With so much time and so little time premium, there's a high likelihood that the option will be prematurely exercised. If that happens, the spreader will have to buy an amount of XYZ stock equivalent to the number of Puts he sold at $40 per share. He will then either have to pay for the stock in the cash or the margin account, or sell the stock in the open market, or sell the stock by exercising the February 35 Puts that he owns. Regardless of his course of action, the spread is involuntarily unwound and substantial additional commission charges are incurred. The approximate commission charge to initially sell five Puts for 5⅜ points is $85, plus another $55 to initially buy the five February 35s at 1⅝. The approximate charge involved in buying 500 shares of XYZ at $40 from the Put exercise would be on the order of another $300. Selling the stock out at some price less than $40 would involve roughly another $300. All these commissions amount to $740. The spreader would be very lucky if he wasn't hit with a loss, possibly a very serious one.

SELLING NAKED PUTS

Notwithstanding all of the above, logic dictates that selling naked Puts in a bull market should be profitable. However, good judgment mediates against selling deep-in-the-money Puts. The best practice is to sell Puts that are somewhat out-of-the-money. The May 30 Puts on XYZ for ⅞ point with the stock at 34¾ (refer to Table 10) would be a reasonable naked sale candidate. If the bull market doesn't materialize (or maybe it does, but XYZ isn't included), the Put will still expire even if the stock were to fall back 4¾ points. With a stable or upwardly biased market, this Put has a good probability of expiring.

Selling naked options of either type has frequently been termed the art of *taking unlimited risk for small profits.* This is not a wholly inaccurate description, except that it ignores the *advantageous probabilities* of selling naked options. Nonetheless, in the hands of the unsophisticated, selling naked Puts can be dangerous. The investor should be well capitalized and able to *comfortably* afford the risk. Many brokerage firms require that an account must have an equity of $10,000 to be qualified for selling naked options.

Basically, *naked Puts are more treacherous than naked Calls* because bear markets traditionally occur with much greater velocity than bull markets. There's a whole herd of profit takers to temper a market advance, but only a handful of stock short-sellers to cushion a collapse. If one sold the XYZ May 35 Put for $2\frac{5}{8}$ points when the stock was at $34\frac{3}{4}$, he would realize $2\frac{3}{8}$ per share of premium over and above the $\frac{1}{4}$ per share of intrinsic value. However, in the last decade's stock market environment, both you and I have seen stocks at this price level sell off as much as $6 in only a few days. Having to pay $35 for a stock worth less than $29 can be a pretty expensive affair, regardless of the time premium received from the option's sale. If one waits for the market to improve, the naked Put seller might be faced with paying $35 for a $24 stock. Of course, as an alternative, he can buy back his Put before the stock is put to him. But the magnitude of the loss will still be essentially the same.

In a peculiar way, the preceding also highlights that naked Puts are *theoretically* less risky than naked Calls. The *maximum* loss that can be realized from selling a Put with a 35 strike price is $35 per share without taking into account commission costs. The stock cannot trade for less than zero. On the other hand, if one were naked a Call, the risk borders on *infinity* since the stock, and the naked Call seller's liability, can rise to virtually any price.

My suggestion is to *guardedly* disregard this theoretical consideration. No intelligent investor, or speculator either, should ever let a loss amount to some theoretical, terminal level. This is particularly true for an investor trading naked options. Just be aware that naked Puts are very risky.

The margin requirement for a short Put position is identical with that for a short Call position. The calculation is not the easiest in the world to remember, but it's well worth the effort. There's a hidden lever, a particular advantage in dealing with options, that might not be altogether obvious at first reading. I'll point it out before this section is concluded.

The requirement is 30 percent of the price of the underlying stock, *plus* the amount the option is in-the-money, or *less* the amount the option is out-of-the-money. This *margin* requirement is then reduced by the proceeds from the sale of the option to determine the *cash* requirement.

Regardless of these calculations, there is a minimum margin requirement of $250.

Table 11   Requirement for a Naked in-the-Money Put (commissions not included)

Sell One XYZ May 40 Put @ 5¾ with Stock @ 34¾

30% × $3,475	$1,042
Plus in-the-money	525
Margin requirement	1,567
Less option proceeds	575
Cash requirement	992

Requirement for a Naked Out-of-the-Money Put (commissions not included)

Sell One XYZ May 30 Put @ ⅞ with Stock @ 34¾

30% × $3,475	$1,042
Less out-of-the-money	475
Margin requirement	567
Less proceeds	87
Cash requirement	480

If you have not been thoroughly convinced that leverage works both ways, observe the impact of marking-to-the-market in an adverse market move. Let us calculate the additional money required to support the naked May 30 Put if the stock drops to $29:

30% of $2,900	$870
Plus in-the-money	100
Margin requirement	970

The initial cash requirement was only $480, but, because of the roughly 6 point adverse move in the stock, the revised requirement generated by the stock's decline is slightly more than doubled to $970 for an increase of $490.

Throughout the margin and cash requirement discussion for both Put bull spreads and naked Puts, the subject of a debit balance has not been brought up. I am going to separately address it at this point because it deserves special attention. Buying Calls or Call bull spreads requires cash. If the cash isn't already in the account or isn't deposited within one day, the cash can be borrowed in the margin account using *other* marginable securities as collateral. In this case, the broker would lend the money and, of course, charge interest on the borrowed money.

However, when employing Put bull spreads or naked Puts, new cash actually flows into the account as a result of the option position. I have already pointed out that this cash reduces the margin requirement. The fascinating aspect of the resulting cash requirement is that it can be met with account equity as well as cash. If other securities are in the account that are not margined either at all or at least not up to the initial margin requirement for those stocks or bonds, this free equity can be used as a substitute for cash. No money is borrowed and no interest is charged. An investor can use the equity value of bonds, debentures, and preferred stock to secure naked Puts and Put bull spreads as well as a number of strategies yet to be mentioned (Call bear spreads, naked Calls, and a variety of ratio speads) without ever borrowing a penny from his broker or ever depositing cash. The fly in the ointment is that the investor must be both prepared and willing to either sell some of his securities, use them as collateral for a margin loan, or bring in fresh money if the particular option strategy runs against him.

AN ADDED WRINKLE—SYNTHETIC STOCK

Combining the purchase of a Call with the sale of the Put having the same exercise price and expiration results in an option construction known as "synthetic" stock. The name is appropriate in that the strategy participates in *all* the *rewards* and *risks* associated with the underlying common stock while markedly reducing initial cash and equity requirements.

The maximum profit that can be realized from a naked Put is the proceeds received from the option's sale. On the other hand, the owner of a Call option can realize a theoretically unlimited profit. Using the cash received from selling the Put to help buy the Call drops the cash required for the Call to a fraction. Going back to our XYZ standby and working with the May 35s, selling the Put for $262.50 would reduce the Call price of $325 to $62.50 before commissions. This $62.50 before commissions represents a remarkably small investment to control 100 shares of a $35 stock. Of course, there is an equity requirement to secure the naked Put. As you have already seen, that is 30 percent of the price of the stock plus a small in-the-money adjustment for the May 35 Put. If one were to buy XYZ outright instead of the "synthetic" stock, the initial margin requirement would be *50 percent* and interest must be *paid* on the debit balance. With "synthetic" stock the equity requirement is only *30 percent* and the equity can be already invested in some other interest or dividend *earning* instrument.

Since options' biggest abuse is *overuse*, I will caution you again. No more "synthetic" stock should be bought using this options strategy than one would normally buy outright. Leverage is a delight when it works, and a financial heartbreak when it doesn't.

5

The Bear Market

The introduction of Puts, albeit on a limited list of securities, represents a dramatic investment opportunity that has heretofore been denied. For a variety of reasons, psychological, political, and sociological, the bearish side of the stock market has been virtually ignored. While the market trend has undeniably been up for the long term from the mid-thirties to 1970, it has frequently been punctuated by some staggering reversals that have occasionally lasted several years. These black clouds have been viewed simply as some inevitable, *minor* ebb in the *major flow* of market history.

Profiting from a decline in prices has been construed as an evil akin to picking a dying man's pockets. The establishment whips itself up to a moral fervor over the baseness of short selling. While the government hasn't made the practice illegal, it has labored mightily to make selling short difficult (the "uptick" rule) and financially less rewarding than it would otherwise be, by an unfavorable tax treatment. (All short sale profits are taxed as short term capital gains regardless of the duration of the position.)

Put options provide an investment vehicle with many advantages over the short sale during a period of declining prices. Using any one of several strategies, Puts require much less capital, offer controlled risk, and are not subject to any uptick limitation when they are either bought or sold.

PUTS VERSUS THE SHORT SALE

Put options are similar to a short sale in that a profit is made in a declining market. However, there are several significant differences. A short sale is the sale of a stock that one doesn't own, but borrowed from another investor who does own the stock, with the idea of buying back the stock at a lower price. A Put is the *right* to sell the stock, but not the accomplished fact. This is a very important distinction. *The Put buyer, should the market advance contrary to his expectations, only has at risk the cost of his Put option. Should the market price of the stock be higher than the strike price of his Put option at expiration, his Put will expire worthless.* If one owns a Put on XYZ stock at 30 with the stock trading at 35, the right to sell a $35 stock for $30 is about as valuable as a three-legged dog. The short seller of the same stock, however, would lose one dollar per share for every one dollar advance and theoretically has an unlimited risk.

Compounding the short seller's risk of an adverse upward price move is his responsibility for dividends on the stock he borrowed to make his short sale. The buyer of the borrowed stock takes possession and is entitled to his dividends. Consequently, the borrower of the stock (the short seller) must pay to the lender any and all dividends to which he is entitled to receive from the corporation. The cost to maintain a short sale for any length of time can be quite significant for a high yielding stock. *However, the owner of a Put, since he merely has the right to sell stock at the strike price of the option, has no obligation to pay a dividend to a stock lender. Hence, he has no carrying charges while he waits for his expectations to become reality.* Nonetheless, he owns a wasting asset, the time premium which will gradually erode as the expiration date of the option draws near. While the stock short seller will profit dollar for dollar with the stock's decline, the Put holder must first recapture the premium paid before he will realize a profit.

The last major distinction between a Put option and a short sale of stock relates to pricing levels. *A short sale must always be made at the prevailing market price at the time of the transaction.* In fact, because of the uptick rule, one can only sell short on an uptick (a price higher than the previous trade) or a zero-plus tick (the same price as the previous trade which was higher than the trade before it). One cannot sell short at a price substantially either higher than or lower than the going market for the subject stock. While a statement that one can't sell a stock at a price for either more or less than it is worth in the marketplace might seem potentially obvious, such is not the case with Put options.

Put options to sell stock both at a higher price than the market and a lower price than the market will usually be trading. And there is no uptick rule which restricts either the sale or the purchase of a Put to any previous trading price.

To repeat my earlier discussion of Puts, a Put with a strike price higher than the current stock price is an in-the-money Put as contrasted to Calls. As an example, a Put option to sell one hundred shares of a $35 stock at $40 must be intrinsically worth at least $500. Conversely, a Put option to sell one hundred shares of this same $35 stock at $30 is out-of-the-money. It has no intrinsic value in and of itself. Of course, the option will trade at some price representing pure time premium as long as there's time and some possibility that there *might* be a profit to be made. At this point it might be helpful for you to refer back to Table 2 to familiarize yourself with this discussion.

PUT PRICING

Historically, Puts have never been as highly valued as Calls. Investors on balance tend to be an optimistic lot. This is one reason why every bear market episode, like the advent of winter, surprises the average investor, both individual and institutional alike. Also, the market has been in one long, discontinuous uptrend for the last three decades.

Consequently, Puts have traditionally been cheaper than Calls. If one bought a straddle (a Put and a Call, each with the same strike price and expiration) in the over-the-counter market, the rule of thumb for tax purposes is to assign 55 percent of the total price to the Call and the other 45 percent to the Put. However, there are several reasons why this old rule of thumb will not hold true in describing the price relationship between Exchange traded Puts and Calls.

With over-the-counter Puts and Calls, dividends paid on the stock under option resulted in a downward adjustment of the strike price of both Put and Call contracts. The effect was to indirectly give the Call holder the benefit of any dividends while a Put holder was penalized by a like amount. When Exchange traded Calls came into being, it was decided not to make any strike price adjustments for dividends paid on the underlying stock. Thus, the buyer of stock and the seller of covered Calls receives full credit for the dividends and the buyer of those Calls does not participate either directly or indirectly in such dividends. Consequently, sellers of Calls find it still economical to write Call options at a lower premium than historical practice, particularly on high-yielding stocks. Since the Call buyer does not have his strike price favorably adjusted for a dividend, he conversely will not bid up the price. And so premium levels have declined on listed Calls, relative to the over-the-counter market for the same option.

The reverse of this logic applies to listed Puts. A buyer of listed Puts would be willing to pay more for an option that will not have an unfavorable strike price adjustment. The Put seller who hedges by selling short the stock will demand a higher price for a Put, since he is responsible for the dividends on the stock sold short. Thus, the price of Puts on high-yielding stocks will rise.

It should also be mentioned that it is very unlikely that large institutions will be sellers of Puts to nearly the extent they are of Calls. While acquiring a stock by writing naked Puts represents buying the stock at a discount equivalent to the Put premium, many institutions will be precluded from this strategy because, on the day the stock is Put to them, they might have to pay more than the prevailing market price. While sophisticated investors will sell Puts to increase their portfolio cash flow, particularly in a rising market, in the aggregate they will not represent as large a selling pressure as currently exists in Calls.

The overall impact of these external forces results in a mixed pricing picture. Added to these is the dominant internal influence of the professional arbitrager.

An arbitrager is an individual or firm, usually a member of the appropriate exchanges, who develops *riskless* positions to capitalize on *small* price discrepancies. Invariably, his commission costs are virtually negligible compared to the charges at the retail level. The arbitrager is a well-capitalized professional.

At any moment, there's always a precise mathematical relationship between the prices of the Puts and Calls on the same underlying stock. If one knows the price of the common and the Call option on the stock, the exact value of the Put corresponding to the Call can be calculated.

The arbitrage coin has two faces. On one side, the arbitrager buys stock, buys a Put, and sells the Call with the same strike price. On the other side, he sells short stock, sells a Put, and buys the Call with the same strike price as the Put. Either configuration is essentially *riskless*.

As an example, let's again refer to XYZ at 34¾ and the February 35 options. The Call is 1⅞ and the Put 1⅝. The long stock version of the arbitrage has historically been termed a "conversion." In the trade it's known as a "forward." The arbitrager buys the stock, buys the February 35 Put and sells the February 35 Call. If the stock declines, it can still be sold at $35 by exercising the Put. If XYZ advances, the stock will assuredly be called away at $35. This conversion is completely riskless at the quoted prices. Additionally, it has a positive return on investment.

Here's how the numbers work. If the stock is called away by the Call being exercised on the arbitrager or is Put by the arbitrager by exercising his Put, he is guaranteed a ¼ point profit no matter which way the stock moves. The Put cost him 1⅝ points, but the 1⅞ points he receives from selling the Call gives him another profit of ¼ point. His total riskless return is ½ point plus any dividend he might get in the next two months. This is on an investment of 34¾. A ½ point return in two months is equivalent to an 8.6 percent annual return. Added to this is a 4.2 percent dividend rate earned by XYZ (the dividend rate of the real stock disguised as XYZ) for a total return of 12.8 percent. At the time these prices were selected, treasury bills were returning 10.5 percent with the prime rate at 11.5 percent. If the arbitrager had to pay 11.5 percent to borrow money on which he could earn 12.8 percent, he would have only marginal interest in this conversion. However, increased conversion activity would be triggered whenever Call prices rise relative to the Puts.

On the other hand, if Call prices dropped relative to the price of Puts, the arbitrager would enter into a *reconversion*. In the trade, this tactic is called a "reverse." Here he would sell short the stock at 34¾, sell the February 35 Put for 1⅝ and buy the February 35 Call for 1⅞. If the stock declines, the Put will be exercised on him at 35 and he will cover his short with the stock for a ¼ point loss. If the stock advances, he will exercise his Call at 35, cover his short sale, and again come up with a ¼ point loss. In addition, the proceeds from the sale of the Put fall short by ¼ point compared to the cost of the Call. Another ¼ point loss. Unlike the converter who realizes a *positive cash flow* from his market positions and dividends earned, the reconverter is faced with *costs*. Being short stock, he's also responsible for the dividends on his borrowed stock. As you can now see, the reconverter must pay a cost that is exactly equal to the converter's return.

If you are curious about why an arbitrager might be eager to lose money, consider the last piece of the puzzle. A reconverter usually has a large quantity of stock that he can borrow freely. A brokerage house can use securities left on deposit by customers. When it borrows these shares and sells them short, it acquires free cash. Depending upon the cost of capital from the banks, the gigantic quantities of cash available from reconverting can be quite enticing.

The object of presenting the workings of the professional arbitragers who operate beyond the pale of the ordinary speculator is to demonstrate that the relative prices of Puts and Calls is really quite rational. When the speculative public becomes enthusiastically bullish and bids up the price of Calls, the price of Puts will expand as converters sell Calls and buy Puts. Conversely, as Calls decline in value, the arbitragers will reconvert by buying Calls and selling Puts to again bring the two types of options into a logical realignment revolving around the prevailing interest rate structure.

BUYING PUTS

Just like Call options, Puts can be used for a variety of ends, some speculative and some conservative. Whether a Put is bought or sold does not in itself dictate that the transaction is necessarily prudent or aggressive. The character depends upon the purpose and strategy into which the Put is incorporated. The purchase of a Put is speculative in just the same manner as buying a Call. *For a lesser sum of money than that required to margin a short sale, the holder profits from a decline in the price of the underlying stock.* He can reap this profit by buying stock at the lower open market price and exercise his option (Putting the stock) at the higher option strike price. Rather than pay the commission to buy stock and then "Put" it, the more usual practice will be simply to sell the Put in the Exchange secondary market. Of course, if the stock goes up or just doesn't fall, the option holder can lose all or most of his investment.

Selecting the most appropriately leveraged Put within the framework of the timing and the magnitude of the expected stock decline requires the exact same analysis as one would make if buying a Call. Rather than repeat the derivation of this reward/risk calculation, I would suggest that you review the Call buying section in Chapter 4.

I've indicated before that Puts tend to respond differently to market fluctuations than do Calls, particularly in-the-money Puts. The speculator buying out-of-the-money or at-the-money Puts will find that, if the underlying stock declines and his option begins to have intrinsic value, his option will increase in price more slowly than would be the case with a profitable Call. In-the-money Puts tend to lose their time premium much more rapidly than Calls. They become sluggish and less responsive to favorable movements of the underlying stock.

Given the forces operating in the market, such behavior is really not peculiar. As I've mentioned, the public does not avidly buy Puts. And although the institutions are not as heavy sellers of Puts as they are Calls, the arbitragers are active sellers as part of their reconversion activity. In times of high interest rates and tight money, reconversion is a source of ample cash.

BEAR SPREADING WITH CALLS

Call options are inherently suited for a bull market. For stocks without Puts, the Call bear spread is one strategy for capitalizing on a downward move.

The bear spread is a vertical spread just as is the bull spread. The options employed have the same expiration date. The Call bear spread consists of buying the at-the-money Call and selling the next lower in-the-money Call.

Table 12   Call Bear Spread XYZ @ 34¾

Strike Price	February (2 mo.)	May (5 mo.)
40	⅜R	1¼
35	Buy 1⅞	Buy 3¼
30	Sell 5⅝	Sell 6¼

The most obvious feature of the Call bear spread is that it is a *credit* spread. It generates cash because the proceeds from the Call sale exceed the cost of the option bought. This cash is the maximum profit that can be earned.

Were the stock to act perversely and run up to any price higher than $35, the 30 Call might well be exercised on the spreader. In such an instance, the spreader always has the alternative of exercising his 35 Call to get the shares that he must deliver at $30. This $5 per share loss would be offset by the credit received when the spread was sold. The difference between the two is the *risk* associated with the spread. We'll ignore the commission costs for a moment.

Examining Table 12, you will find that the credit received for the February bear spread is 3¾ before commissions and 3 points for the May spread. This means that the *risk* is 1¼ points for the February and 2 points for the May. While the point difference might not seem tremendous, in percentage terms it is quite significant. As with the bull spreads already studied, the reward/risk parameters are *always more attractive with* the *more nearby* expiration date spreads than with the deferred. The reason is obvious. The option bought is almost always pure time premium while the option sold has high intrinsic value and little time premium. The more distant at-the-money option carries an increasing amount of time premium compared to the in-the-money component of the spread. Thus, the risk is always higher and the reward correspondingly lower.

The reward/risk ratio, as seen in Table 13, is tremendously more attractive for the February spread with two months to

Table 13   Five Lot Call Bear Spread Reward/Risk (before and after approximate commissions)

	February Expiration				May Expiration			
Strike Price	Option Price	Gross Price	Approx. Comm.	Net Price	Option Price	Gross Price	Approx. Comm.	Net Price
35	1⅞	$ 937	+60	$ 997	3¼	$1,625	+70	$1,695
30	5⅝	$2,812	−85	$2,727	6¼	$3,125	−90	$3,035
Reward/Risk		3.00		2.25		1.50		1.15

run, versus the May with five months. This is very characteristic of this species. And this feature, of course, limits the strategy to *traders only*. There is no long-term potential with Call bear spreads.

Table 13 also makes a powerful statement about the dangers of taking an oversimplistic approach to spreads. *The attractiveness of any spread should always be judged after commissions are taken into account.* Commission costs are a very appreciable cost and can turn a seemingly profitable spread into a fiasco. If your broker suggests a trade, make him go through the drill of figuring it out after commissions. Also, the commission costs I have used do not adhere to any brokerage firm's schedule. They are approximate. If you shop around, you'll find some firms' charges are less, some are more. *Spreaders beware!*

Which subject brings up the *Call bear spread trap*. Being short the in-the-money Call is a constant invitation to a premature exercise of the option. The *maximum* possible profit on a five lot February spread is $2,727 less $997, or $1,730. The commission cost to buy and sell 500 shares of stock would run around $500, an enormous bite out of the best possible profit. All in all, the Call bear spread is a fair-to-middling strategy if there are no Puts available. It is rotten if there are.

THE PUT BEAR SPREAD

As strategies go, this one harmonizes beautifully with the market's dynamics. Just like the Call bear spread, it consists of buying the at-the-money option and selling the lower strike price option.

Since the option sold is well out-of-the-money, there is no likelihood of a premature exercise forcing the spread into involuntary liquidation. No extra commission for the spreader, and he retains control of his market position until he decides to liquidate.

The out-of-the-money Puts he sells are cheap, but then so are the at-the-money Puts he buys.

Table 14 Put Bear Spread XYZ @ 34¾

Strike Price	February (2 mo.)	May (5 mo.)
40	5⅜	5¾
35	Buy 1⅝	Buy 2⅝
30	Sell ¼	Sell ⅞

Because the options dealt with in the spread are relatively low priced, the effect of commissions is less. If you will refer back to Table 13, you will see that the February Call bear spread looked quite attractive before commissions, but after commissions on a five lot spread was no better than the Put bear spread.

SELLING NAKED CALLS

Selling a Call on a stock not owned is termed naked because one does not have the stock to cover the obligation to deliver stock in the event the option is exercised. The naked Call seller must step into the market and buy the necessary stock at whatever price he must pay to secure the shares he must deliver.

Being short a Call has all the advantages and disadvantages of being long a Call, *but exactly in reverse.* A speculator who is short a Call has only limited prospects for gain and unlimited loss potential. Using the May 35 Call at 3¼ with XYZ trading at 34¾ as an example, the naked seller can only realize $3.25 per share even if XYZ were to plummet to $25. Since the whole rationale of selling short is to buy back at a lower price a security previously sold at a higher price, the lowest price at which this 3¼ point option can be bought back is zero. If one had

Table 15 Five Lot Put Bear Spread Reward/Risk
(before and after approximate commission costs)

Strike Price	Option Price	Gross Price	Approx. Comm.	Net Price	Option Price	Gross Price	Approx. Comm.	Net Price
35	1⅝	$812	+60	$872	2⅝	$1,323	+65	$1,377
30	¼	$125	−25	$100	⅞	$ 438	−45	$ 393
Reward/Risk		2.64		2.25		1.86		1.55

sold short the XYZ common, instead of the Call, the potential profit would be a little less than $10 per share. On the other hand, if XYZ had moved upward, there would be no limit to the amount of money that either the short seller of a Call or the common could lose.

With such seemingly appalling disadvantages, why would a speculator sell naked Calls? Actually there are several sound reasons for certain qualified investors to use this strategy.

The first reason is ease. When selling short stock, the stock must first be borrowed so that certificates can be delivered when the stock is sold, and that sale can only be done on an uptick, i.e., in an advancing market. An option short seller faces neither of these problems. Listed options trade by bookkeeping entries. There are no certificates involved and thus none have to be borrowed to make delivery. Also, there are no uptick requirements for selling short options. An option can be sold short when the market is falling to the seller's advantage.

Secondly, the overall trading statistics, which indicate that only one Call in five expires with a profit, works to the advantage of the naked seller. Unlike the stock short seller who must see his stock *decline* to make money, the option short seller will make money if the stock just *doesn't go up too much*. If XYZ is still at 34¾ on the third Friday in May, the May 35 Call will expire and the naked seller will realize his full 3¼ point profit. In fact, if the stock rises to some price less than 38¼ from 34¾ by the expiration date of the option, *some* profit will still be made, neglecting commissions.

If the naked seller used the May 40 Call at 1¼ rather than the May 35 Call, he would realize his full $125 per option before commissions as long as XYZ doesn't get up to $40. The naked seller is banking against a dramatic price rise in some defined period of time, and the probabilities are usually in his favor.

The last major reason for selling naked Calls is financial leverage. Were XYZ common sold short, the current margin requirement according to Regulation T of the Federal Reserve would be 50 percent of the market price of the stock. Selling short 100 shares of XYZ at $35 would require $1,750 and $1,737 at 34¾. This initial margin requirement is the same as that required for buying stock on margin.

The margin requirement for the naked option is *30 percent* of the market value of the underlying stock adjusted for a difference between the strike price of the option sold and the current price of the stock. This is further reduced by the proceeds from the sale of the option. And, as I've already pointed out, the option requirement pertains to an equity requirement, not money that must be borrowed. The requirement of the May 35 with the stock at 34¾ would be 30 percent of $3,475 or $1,042 less $25 for the ¼ point difference between the strike price and the stock price. The option proceeds would further reduce the requirement by another $325 to $692.

The margin requirement for the May 40 Call at 1¼ would still be 30 percent of the stock price for 100 shares, or $1,042, as in the above case. As an out-of-the-money option, the difference between the stock and the strike price, the 5¼ points, reduces the requirement by $525 to $517. (Were the option sold in-the-money, this difference between stock and strike price would be added to the initial calculation.) The option proceeds of $125 further reduces the equity requirement to $392. Regardless of the calculation, the *minimum* requirement for any option is

Table 16   Financial Leverage of Naked Calls
(commission costs excluded)

	Short XYZ @ 34¾	Naked May 35 @ 3¼	Naked May 40 @ 1¼
Margin requirement	$1,737	$692	$392
Profit if stock unchanged at expiration	—	325	125
Profit if stock declines $10 by expiration	1,000	325	125
Profit if stock advances $5 by expiration	−500	−175	125
Profit if stock advances $10 by expiration	−1,000	−675	−325

$250. In addition, the Options Clearing Corporation requires that a naked seller must have a minimum account equity of $2,000. Most brokerage firms have a much higher minimum equity account size for naked sellers.

The stock short seller is responsible to the party from whom he borrowed the stock for any dividends paid on the borrowed stock. The option short seller has no such liability, since options don't pay dividends.

The naked Call has considerable leverage over the short sale in that it can return a much greater percentage profit on invested capital for much smaller changes in the price of the underlying stock. This is true even to the extent that an unprofitable short sale can still be a profitable option short sale on the same stock as long as the stock does not advance too far beyond the strike price of the option sold short.

However, the other edge of the leverage sword cuts deeply if both shorted stock and the corresponding options move up sharply. A speculator short the stock will lose $100 per 100 shares for every $1 advance in the stock. The speculator short options will also lose $100 per option for every $1 advance in the *option, plus* he will have to post additional equity to the account equivalent to 130 percent of the underlying stock's advance.

Selling out-of-the-money naked Calls is quite like going short at a price higher than the market. The naked seller doesn't have to be right—*just not too wrong!* Nonetheless, this strategy should only be used by sophisticated investors who can follow their positions closely. And still there is risk. My advice is to stay with the out-of-the-money Calls as naked selling candidates. You should also select the nearby Calls. The options sold are all time premium. The nearer the expiration, the more quickly the seller will earn his premium, and, the less time, the lower the probability of an adverse price movement.

THE SYNTHETIC SHORT SALE

Just as it is possible to fashion an options posture that closely approximates the risk and reward characteristics of owning common stock, the same is true for matching the short sale with options. In fact, the option construction is *superior* in several important features and should *always be employed instead of* the *short sale* when the listed options are available.

Stock short sellers seldom hold their position for the long term. The technique is aggressive and almost exclusively used by traders trying to cash in on an abrupt downward swing. Also, paying out the dividends on the short can get expensive. However, the "synthetic" short sale can be put on for at least six months at the minimum. This is one of the *few* option *strategies* which *does not increase* in either *cost* or *risk as* the *more deferred* option *expiration options are employed.*

As you can see in Table 17, the proceeds from the sale of the Call are more than the cost of the Put. No cash is required for the trade (before commissions), just sufficient account equity to adequately margin the naked Call. Of course, these price relationships would vary if the underlying stock were not quite as close to the strike price of the options.

The risk of the position is the same as that encountered with the short sale of stock. If XYZ advances instead of declining over the life of the options, the Put that was bought will expire and the naked Call can become a virtually infinite liability. A speculator can only be comfortable with either a short sale or a "synthetic" short sale if he has iron-willed discipline. When the position is established, he fixes in his mind the total amount of risk he is willing to expose himself to. If the position reaches that level, he closes it out without any temporizing. Either he, his broker, or both must watch the trade like a hawk to make sure the fuse is crimped before a fatal explosion.

Table 17   "Synthetic" Sale XYZ @ 34¾

	Strike Price	February (2 mo.)	May (5 mo.)	August (8 mo.)
Sell Calls	35	1⅞	3¼	4⅜
Buy Puts	35	1⅝	2⅝	3⅜

From the reward standpoint, if XYZ declines the naked Call will expire and the long Put will increase in value very nearly dollar for dollar with the stock's slump. The potential profit is limited to the extent that the stock can only drop to zero and no farther. Also, there is no carrying cost for the "synthetic" because there is no dividend liability.

The return on investment for the "synthetic" is much better than that for the real short sale assuming an equal drop in the stock. The short sale initial margin requirement is *50 percent* of the market value of the stock while the naked Call requirement is computed on *30 percent* of the market value with the appropriate in-the-money or out-of-the-money adjustment. Normally, a deep-in-the-money Put would not be bought, because this would increase both the risk and the cash required for the trade.

Table 17 would prompt one to use the most deferred options for the "synthetic" short sale, since the difference between the Call sold and the Put bought is the widest with the August series. This extra cash inflow reduces the equity requirement a bit. Least requirement, longest time—an unbeatable combination? *Not really.* From a practical standpoint, these most deferred options are the most difficult to trade. The bulk of speculative activity tends to flow to the nearby options. The lesser trading volume in the deferred options almost always reduces liquidity. The price spreads between bid and ask are wider, making it more difficult to trade at the desired price with the desired number of contracts. If putting on a position is slow and laborious, *beware!* You might have more patience getting in, and considerably less if you are trying to beat a hasty retreat from a destructive bull market spurt. Be *very cautious* about overcommitting to an illiquid position.

6

Neutral Market Strategies

There are times when the investor perceives that the market of stocks (or maybe a group of stocks, or just one individual stock) is in the doldrums. There seems to be a low likelihood of any significant movement either up or down. Possibly a few points one way or the other, but all in all a rather trendless affair. Using strategies that require a definite trend to be effective when the market has the "blahs" is both frustrating and expensive. Fortunately, there are a variety of option techniques that function very well with relatively stagnant prices.

THE ALLIGATOR—THE TIME SPREAD

Thus far, all the spreads we have studied are *vertical;* the options involved all have the same expiration. The time spread is *horizontal.* It involves buying and selling options with different expiration dates. The Option Clearing Corporation provides favorable margin treatment for horizontal spreads on the condi-

Table 18   Time Spreads with Strike Price 35 Options
XYZ @ 34¾

	February (2 mo.)	May (5 mo.)	August (8 mo.)
Call	1⅞	3¼	4⅜
Put	1⅝	2⅝	3⅜

tion that options sold short must be secured by an equal number of long options on the same underlying stock which expire at the *same* time or at a *later* date than the short options.

The time spread involves selling short the nearby option and buying the same strike price option of the next farther out expiration date. The idea is to sell the time premium in the nearby option, which will disappear completely if the option expires, while taking a smaller loss in value in the long option which still has considerable life left. Because the object is to sell short an option that has lots of premium, time spreading usually deals with at-the-money options.

Let's first walk through with a Call time spread. Selling the February 35 for 1⅞ points and paying 3¼ points for the May Call would require 1⅜ points of new cash over and above the proceeds received from the February 35 sale. All before commissions, of course.

If the stock does not move at all in the next two months, the February Call would expire for a gain of 1⅞. However, the May option would also be expected to decline somewhat, say to the same price as the February option when the spread was put on. Going from 3¼ to 1⅞ would represent a loss of 1⅜ points. Losing 1⅜ while making 1⅞ represents a profit of ½ point on the above defined investment of 1⅜ points.

Sell 5 February 35 Calls @ 1⅞	=	$ 937.50
less approximate commission of		60.00
		877.50
Buy 5 May 35 Calls @ 3¼	=	$1,625.00
plus approximate commission of		70.00
		1,695.00

Is this spread worth the bother? What are the real, total costs of the time spread, after commissions?

If the February 35 Call expires, the spreader is ahead $877.50. The market value of his May 35 Call would drop, according to the above scenario, to about 1⅞, which would be a dollar decline of his $1,695 investment to $937.50 (an unrealized loss of $757.50). If he sells these Calls at 1⅞, the loss increases by the $60 commission to $817.50. Under ideal conditions, the Call time spreader would realize a $60 profit ($877.50 less $817.50) on a five lot spread on a before commission investment of 1⅜ points times five or $687.50. Annualize the $180 profit made in two months on the investment and the result is a respectable 52 percent—*if the spread works perfectly.*

If XYZ advances instead of staying in limbo, the least that can happen is that the difference in price between the two options will *narrow* instead of *expanding* the anticipated ½ point. If the differential doesn't expand, the $60 profit turns into a loss. The worst that can happen is that the February 35 will be exercised on the spreader and he will have to exercise his May 35 Call to come up with the stock. The two exercises on 500 shares can cost in excess of $550 in commissions over and above the complete loss of the spread differential.

If, instead of advancing, XYZ moves down from the 34¾ level, the value of the long May 35 Call is threatened by an eroding price. If the spreader doesn't sell out promptly, he could lose a good part, or all, of his invested capital.

Going through the same drill using a Put time spread demonstrates that Puts are marginally preferred as vehicles for time spreads.

Sell 5 February Puts @ 1⅝	=	$ 812.50
less approximate commission of		60.00
		752.50
Buy 5 May 35 Puts @ 2⅝	=	$1,312.50
plus approximate commission of		65.00
		1,377.50

The cash required for this five lot spread is the difference between sale proceeds and the purchase cost, or $625.

If XYZ were to uptick just a tad on the February expiration date so that the February 35 Put expires, there will be a realized gain on this short option of $752.50. Assuming that in the meantime the May 35 Put declines from 2⅝ to 1⅝, there will be an unrealized loss on the May 35 Put of $1,377.50 less $812.50 or $565. Combining the gains and the losses on the two positions we come up with an ideal profit of $752.50 less $565 or $187.50. This ideal profit is better than could be obtained with Calls on a slightly lesser investment. Nonetheless, the Put time spread is threatened with all the same hazards as is its Call twin. Either the whole investment can be lost on the one hand, or one can be faced with the horrendous commission charges from exercised options on the other.

Occasionally, time spreads will work on the *big* stocks, i.e., high-priced ones like Teledyne, IBM, or Dupont. This is because there is a sufficiently large difference in the horizontal option's prices to overshadow the impact of the commission costs. However, as a general rule time spreads with either Puts or Calls are *alligators—the commissions will eat you alive.*

I have heard the rationale that time spreads provide access to cheap long options. If the option sold expires and then the stock makes a move favorable to the unexpired long option, the leverage on the long option is greatly magnified. I would advise you to leave this type of double bank shot to "Minnesota Fats." It's difficult enough to foresee a single trend, let alone one that drops and then rises or rises and then drops.

Time spreads are appropriate for the professionals who only pay minor commissions, *not for speculators or investors.*

RATIO SPREADS

The principal risk of owning an option is that, if the underlying stock doesn't move, the time value of the option gradually wastes away, leaving only the taste of ashes. However, you have already seen how this fact of life can be used to reduce the cost and thereby the risk of owning options in the section covering Call bull spreads. With that vertical spread, selling an out-of-the-money Call against each at-the-money option on a one-to-one basis reduced the price of the long Call without increasing the risk.

A flexible variation of this strategy is to sell more out-of-the-money options than are owned at the lower strike price. The number sold compared to the number owned is termed the *ratio*. By overselling the out-of-the-money Calls, the risk of losing money if the stock doesn't move up much, or even at all, can be adjusted. In return for this benefit, the ratio spreader becomes vulnerable if the stock moves up too much. An illustration will be helpful, and we'll ignore commissions for simplicity.

The one-to-one spread is the basic Call bull spread. By selling the one May 40 Call, the spreader reduces his *cost* to two points per spread before commissions. If both options expire, the spreader is out $200 per spread. If XYZ is at $37, two points over the long option's strike price on the third Friday in May, the spreader would break even before commissions.

With a two-to-one ratio, the sale of the extra May 40 Call reduces the cash outlay to ¾ of a point. If all the options expire, the spreader loses ¾ of a point before commissions.

With a three-to-one ratio, there is no cash outlay for the spread. There's a positive cash flow of ½ point before commis-

Table 19   Ratio Spreads—Net Credit In Points

	1 to 1	2 to 1	3 to 1
Sale proceeds from May 40 Calls @ 1¼	1¼	2½	3¾
Cost of May 35 Calls	3¼	3¼	3¼
Net Credit	−2	− ¾	+ ½

Table 20   Call Ratio Spread Downside Breakeven on XYZ (before commissions)

	1 to 1	2 to 1	3 to 1
Downside Breakeven	$37	$35¾	none

sions. If all the options expire because XYZ doesn't move up by May, the spreader would make ½—even if the stock goes to zero.

There's an old saying that goes, "Every once in a while, a hog picks up an acorn." The spreader's "acorn" would be the stock moving just to 40 by expiration date. At that point, the options sold would expire and there would be a profit on the long options.

Now, what happens if the hog chokes on the acorn, if XYZ doesn't stop moving up after it reaches $40. The ratio spreader is unbalanced in market exposure. He is short more options than he owns. Beyond $40, his profit will decline in proportion to the number of options he is short, a break-even point will be reached and then the position will begin to lose money.

There is no upside break-even point for the one-to-one spread. The spreader will make 3 points before commissions, regardless of whether XYZ moves to $45 or $145. The liability of his short May 40 is fully covered by his long May 35.

Table 21   Call Option Ratio Spread
Maximum Profit on XYZ @ 40 (in points
per spread before commissions)

	1 to 1	2 to 1	3 to 1
Proceeds from expired May 40 Calls	1¼	2½	3¾
Profit from May 35 Call (5 −3¼)	1¾	1¾	1¾
Total Profit	3	4¼	5½

Table 22   Call Ratio Spread Upside Breakeven
(before commissions)

	1 to 1	2 to 1	3 to 1
Profit at $40	3 pts.	4¼ pts.	5½ pts.
Uncovered Options	none	1	2
Upside Breakeven $\left(\dfrac{\text{Profit}}{\text{Uncovered Options}}\right) + \$40$	none	44¼	42¾

The two-to-one ratio spreader will lose 1 point in the spread for every 1 point advance in XYZ above $40, the strike price of the one uncovered option.

The three-to-one spreader will lose 2 points in the spread for every 1 point advance in XYZ above $40, because he has two uncovered options working against him.

Having raised the issue of commission costs and their detrimental effect on certain types of spreads, I am pleased to report that ratio spreads are generally not *abnormally* impacted by these transaction costs.

Table 24 was prepared without elaborating on the approximate commission details. Nonetheless, two generalizations about commissions can be made by examining Table 24 compared to Table 23.

Commission costs have the most telling effect when the spread strategy maximum return is relatively small.

All the examples used in the book so far have been in the

Table 23   Summary of Call Ratio Spread Parameters (before commissions)

	1 to 1	2 to 1	3 to 1
Upside Breakeven	none	$44¼	$42¾
Maximum Profit (XYZ @ $40)	3 pts.	4¼ pts.	5½ pts.
Downside Breakeven	$37	$35¾	none

Table 24   Summary of Call Ratio Spread Parameters (after approx. commissions on a five lot spread)

	1 to 1	2 to 1	3 to 1
Upside Breakeven	none	$44	$42½
Maximum Profit (XYZ @ $40)	2¾ pts.	4 pts.	5 pts.
Downside Breakeven	$37¼	$36⅛	none

quantity of five options. Commission costs for any kind of a *one lot* spread are usually prohibitive. In Exhibit 29, a five-by-five lot was set up against a five-by-ten lot, and a five-by-fifteen lot spread. And the result is that commission costs become less important as the number of options involved increases.

The Call ratio spreads used are *mildly* bullish in stance even if the ratio were increased beyond three-to-one. The maximum profit accrues at $40, some $5\frac{1}{4}$ points above the stock price of $34\frac{3}{4}$. Yet, the *band of profitability* can be easily adjusted depending upon the spreader's expectation of XYZ's future. The higher the ratio, the more downside protection. This protection is paid for by an increase in the upside risk. After the initial judgment is made, the ratio spread can be adjusted due to changing circumstances as the market pursues its inexorable course. The experienced trader never *adds* to an existing position. Adjustments should be made *only* if the underlying stock moves counter to expectations. That aspect of the spread which is doing the financial damage should be *reduced* to reflect the revised prospects. Adding to one side by either selling or buying more options invariably *adds to the risk* when the whole purpose of an adjustment is to *reduce* risk.

Ratio spreading is not limited to Calls. The strategy can be just as effective with Puts. However, there are many fewer opportunities with Puts simply because there are fewer stocks on which listed Puts are traded. Also, Put ratio spreads are inherently more treacherous than the Call option variety. Historically, stock prices collapse much more rapidly than they advance. And the *open-ended risk* with a *Put ratio spread* is on the *downside*.

As inviting as the mechanics of the ratio spread might seem, *every* option strategy hinges on the movement of the underlying stock *within a time frame* determined by the expiration of the option. If the expiration cycle selected is nearby, there is liable to be too little time premium in the options sold for the spread to have an attractive band of profitability. If the farthest out expiration cycle is used, an element of control is sacrificed. Time premium is slow to erode on the most distant options and the spread is also more vulnerable to the intrusion of some totally unexpected and destructive disturbance. My recommendation is to work with midrange options having *at least three months* of life but *no more than six months*. High volatility stocks with an enthusiastic speculative following sometimes are advantageous shorter-term prospects because the out-of-the-money Calls can become grossly overpriced.

The margin treatment for a Call ratio spread requires that the spread be separated into its component parts (a bull spread and some number of naked options depending upon the ratio). A two-to-one ratio spread consists of one bull spread and one naked option. In a five lot spread, there are five bull spreads and five naked options. A three-to-one ratio spread done five times consists of five spreads and ten naked options. The cash and equity requirement from each segment is combined for the total requirement.

As an example, I'll use the five lot May two-to-one ratio spread and ignore commissions. The bull spread portion will require $3\frac{1}{4}$ points less $1\frac{1}{4}$, or 2 points per portion. Two points per 100-share option spread is $200. If you multiply by five that means that $1,000 in cash is required for the bull spread. This cash must either be deposited, already in the account, or borrowed in the margin account using some other security as collateral.

As far as the five naked Calls are concerned, the margin requirement is 30 percent of the underlying stock at $34\frac{1}{4}$ or $1,042.50 less $5\frac{1}{4}$ points, or $525 per spread (the out-of-the-money adjustment), for a total of $517.50. If you multiply by five, this margin requirement is $2,587.50.

Combining the two segments, for the five lot spread, the *total* cash requirement is $1,000 for the bull spread less the proceeds from the sale of the naked Calls (five times $1\frac{1}{4}$ points, or $625), for a total of $375. The account must also have $2,587.50 in equity to meet the margin requirement for the naked Calls. As has been pointed out before, there should be plenty of excess equity in the account to meet the refigured requirement for the naked Calls if the stock advances. Every $1 advance towards 40 in XYZ's price will increase the equity requirement by $130 per Call, or $650 for the spread.

THE BUTTERFLY

This spread's name is derived from a somewhat similar strategy first used in the commodity futures market. In the options market, the butterfly is oriented towards a completely neutral or slightly bullish or bearish outlook for the underlying stock. The purpose of the spread is to earn time premium with a precisely determined risk, should the stock move out one way or the other. Structurally vertical, it consists of a bull spread combined with a bear spread. While it is applicable to either Puts or Calls, I'll use the May XYZ Calls as an example. The proportions are long *one* in-the-money, short *two* at-the-money, and long *one* out-of-the-money Call. Any multiple of this proportion can be used.

If XYZ falls below $30 by May, all the options will expire and the loss would be $100 per spread. If XYZ explodes beyond $40, the loss before commissions will again just be $100 per spread. This being the case, the *band of profitability* must be from $31 on the downside to $39 on the upside with a maximum risk of one point per spread. If XYZ is exactly at $40 at the May expiration, the May 40s and the May 35s will expire. The May 30 will be worth five points and can be sold at that price. Since the dollar risk was one point and the maximum selling price is five points, the maximum profit from this spread is $400 before commissions.

Naturally, commission costs will *increase* the *risk* and *decrease* the potential *profit*.

The $775 cash outflow after commissions represents a little

Table 25   Call Butterfly Spread
XYZ @ 34¾ (before commissions)

Strike Price	May (5 mo.)	Butterfly in Points
40	Buy One @ 1¼	−1¼
35	Sell Two @ 3¼	+6½
30	Buy One @ 6¼	−6¼
	Cash Inflow (Outflow)	(−1)

more than 1½ points on the five lot butterfly after approximate commissions. This cash cost is also the risk. Conversely, the potential profit is 3½ points (the difference in option strike prices of life less the 1½ point cost). This makes for a reward/risk ratio of 2.3, all in all an attractive package in a flat market.

The butterfly is the logical extension of a ratio spread whereby a sufficient number of Calls are bought at the strike price just above the one of the short options to balance out the spread. Just as many options are long in the aggregate as are short. While there still might be a loss if the stock doesn't behave as expected, there's no unlimited risk exposure as with the ratio spread.

If one is "legging into" a butterfly, that is, putting on the spread in pieces rather than all in one trade, I recommend starting with the ratio spread portion. Buying the in-the-money Calls and selling the at-the-money Calls in the proper ratio, at the desired prices, is usually the most difficult trade to execute. Once this is completed, the out-of-the-money Calls can then be more leisurely purchased. These Calls are much less sensitive to movements of the underlying stock, and therefore much less likely to "run away" in price before they can be bought.

One last statement before launching into the margin treatment of the butterfly spread. While the calculated risk is one point before commissions, or $775 on a five-lot spread after commissions, it is possible that the risk *could be greater*. Were XYZ to make a large upward thrust, there is the likelihood that the naked May 35 Calls might be prematurely exercised. One thousand shares of XYZ would have to be bought either in the open market or through the exercise of some or all of the long

Table 26   Five Lot Call Butterfly Spread
with XYZ @ 34¾ (after approx. commissions)

Buy 5 May 30 Calls @ 1¼	$ 625	+55	680
Sell 10 May 35 Calls @ 3¼	3,250	−130	3,120
Buy 5 May 30 Calls @ 6¼	3,125	+90	3,215
		Net Cash Outflow	= 775

options for delivery at the May 35 strike price. This loss would be offset by the profit on any of the May 30 and May 40 Calls not exercised. But the commissions for the exercise and the purchase of the shares could run as much as an additional $900 in addition to the calculated risk.

The equity requirement beyond the cash outlay is the combined total of the bull spread portion and the bear spread portion, with each treated separately. The bull spread portion (long one May 30 and short one May 35) only has a cash requirement. There are no equity requirements for a Call bull spread. The Call bear spread (long the May 40 Call at $1\frac{1}{4}$ and short one May 35 at $3\frac{1}{4}$) does have an equity requirement. This is the difference in the strike prices less the proceeds from the sale of the bear spread. On its own, the bear spread generates a 2 point credit ($3\frac{1}{4}$ less $1\frac{1}{4}$). However, these two points are used to offset the cost of the bull spread portion and are not really available in the account. Thus, the equity requirement for the bear spread and for the whole butterfly spread is five points, or $2,500 for the five-lot butterfly.

THE RATIO DIAGONAL SPREAD

I will have to describe this spread in words because the XYZ example is really not a very suitable one. In fact, there are really not very many occasions when the price relationships are available. The place to look for the ratio diagonal spread is among the options on the higher-priced stocks.

The strategy involves selling naked an at-the-money option with about three months of life left. The proceeds from the sale are then used to buy at least two options for each one sold at the next farther out expiration and the next higher strike price. An example would be to sell five February 35 Calls and buy ten May 40 Calls. The problem with the XYZ prices is that the sale proceeds are not enough to buy the diagonal Calls without adding more cash to the pot. But the logic of the spread requires that sufficient cash from the sale must be generated to buy the diagonal Calls.

And here's why. If the stock doesn't move at all during the life of both the nearby and the next farther out Calls, all the options will expire. But there will be no loss because the short option portion paid the long ones.

If the short option expires and the stock then moves up, virtually unlimited profit can be made from the long Calls, which then have a zero cost base.

Should the stock advance after the spread is established, the short option will start producing a loss immediately. The farther out-of-the-money options will start advancing also, but at a slower pace. However, because there are at least twice as many long as short, the total appreciation of these options will keep pace with the short Call loss. If the underlying stock explodes upward, the spread will do handsomely because the net option stance is on the long side.

As I've mentioned, the opportunities for this type of spread are infrequent. So, by definition, this is a trading position suitable only for an aggressive speculator who is just not willing, but actually able to take the inherent risks. Amateurs wait for someone else to point out the game. A professional hunts his own.

The margin treatment for a hybrid spread like the ratio diagonal could conceivably be complicated. In fact, it's quite simple. Even though the options bought have a later expiration than the option sold, the essential risk is that associated with a bear spread. Since all the cash from the short option is eaten up to buy the long options, the margin requirement, and therefore the equity requirement, is the difference in strike prices between the short option and the long option.

THE STRADDLE—THE DOUBLE THREAT

The "double threat" speculative strategy is to buy a straddle. The straddle is a Put and a Call, each with the same exercise and strike price. The idea of the straddle is to make money no matter what direction the stock moves. If the stock moves away from the strike price, either up or down, farther than is required to earn the money paid for the straddle, a profit will be made. Heaven for a straddle buyer is a whipsaw market whereby money can be made on both options. Let us say the stock dives and the holder sells the Put side of his straddle for a profit. If the stock then rebounds, it might be also possible to sell the Call side for an additional profit. The returns can be heady, *IF*, and it is a big if, the stock is sufficiently volatile and the holder has the proper market timing. It's something like pitching a ball, running to the plate, hitting a high fly, and then racing to the outfield to put yourself out. Imagine the same straddle holder selling his Call side on the dip to salvage some of his investment, and then abruptly watching his Put investment disappear on the rally. And don't think that such a foolish scenario hasn't occurred before and won't again.

Indecision and straddles are expensive. Since a straddle can be profitable in either a sharply advancing or declining market, the obvious implication is that the buyer has *no idea* which way the stock will move and is hedging his bet. Because of this uncertainty, the straddle buyer pays almost twice as much for his speculation as he would if he could forecast a specific market direction and then concentrate on either the Put or the Call.

Referring to XYZ, the February 35 straddle (the Call @ 1⅞ and the Put @ 1⅝) represents 10.1 percent of the underlying stock price. The May 35 straddle is 16.9 percent and the August straddle 22.3 percent of the underlying stock. These percentages roughly represent the percent move the stock must make away from the $35 level over the life of the straddle for the owner to *just break even*.

Which topic suggests an interesting alternative to straddle buying. *Selling straddles naked*. If XYZ stays generally around

Table 27   Band of Profitability for Naked Straddles (in points before commissions) XYZ @ 34¾

	Feb.	May	Aug.
Straddle (35 Strike Price)	3½	5⅞	7¾
Upside Breakeven	38½	40⅞	42¾
Downside Breakeven	31½	29⅛	27¼

the $35 level, one side of the straddle will expire, and the time premium in the other will shrink down to the option's intrinsic value as the expiration date draws near.

The band of profitability was simply derived by *adding* the *price* of the straddle to the strike price for the *upside breakeven* point and *subtracting* the straddle *price* from the strike price for the *downside breakeven* point. If XYZ stays within the band, the naked seller will have a profit. Of course, if the stock moves outside the band, the seller could have an unlimited loss, just as the straddle buyer could reap a corresponding profit.

With a fairly wide band of profitability, there is generally a good probability that the naked straddle seller will glean some profit. And a generally low probability that he will be taken to the cleaners. This strategy obviously should *only* be used by the most *sophisticated* and *well financed* speculator.

Short straddles are afforded favorable margin treatment. The margin requirement is calculated for the naked Call side, then the naked Put side. The requirement will be simply the *greater of the two*. They are not added together. In addition, the total proceeds from the sale of the straddle can then be applied to reduce the requirement. As with all naked option requirement calculations, the remaining figure is the equity requirement for the investor's account. While the exchanges insist that the naked seller have at least $2,000 of equity, most brokers require a substantially larger equity.

COMBINATIONS

An alternative to the ordinary straddle is the out-of-the-money spread straddle. This combination of options in the new parlance of the industry is properly called a *combination*, although unofficial terms such as "spreadle" and "strapple" have already sprung up. With the combination, the buyer purchases an out-of-the-money Put and an out-of-the-money Call, each option with the same expiration but with a different strike price. The advantage of the technique for the buyer is the lower cost. The disadvantage to the buyer is that there is a "dead zone" wherein the combination buyer will lose his whole investment. As an example, we can refer to the out-of-the-money May XYZ combination involving the May 40 Call @ 1¼ and the May 30 Put @⅞. If at expiration XYZ is anywhere between $30 and $40, both options will expire worthless.

The *dead band* of this combination naturally works to the combination seller's advantage. The total of the two premiums (1¼ plus ⅞, or 2⅛ points) would be added to the $40 strike price to determine the upper breakeven point of 42⅛, and subtracted from the $30 strike price to calculate the downside breakeven point of 27⅞. This band is somewhat wider than that for the naked May 35 straddle in Table 27, and is correspondingly safer. However, the potential profit (the option proceeds) is also quite a bit less.

If the market is hesitant and not likely to pick up steam in any particular direction, selling naked straddles would be appropriate for the sophisticated investor. If the market is likely to break out after its indecisiveness, selling the naked combination would be less risky. In my view, the aggressive speculator would have a higher profit probability through buying the combination under the same circumstances.

The margin treatment for the combination is identical with that for a naked straddle. Calculate the naked requirement for each side, take the larger, and then subtract the total sale proceeds to come up with the equity requirement.

Combinations can be varied all over the lot. A speculator can buy an in-the-money Call and an out-of-the-money Put or vice versa. In addition, he isn't limited to a one-to-one ratio between the two types of options. He can load up one side or the other depending on his judgment of the future direction of the stock's price. Any way you cut it, there's virtually an infinite number of combinations in which listed Puts and Calls can be arrayed. The only limit is the speculator's imagination.

7

Future Prospects

In early 1975, in the conclusion to my book *Options Trading*, I predicted that options trading volume might increase to 50,000 contracts per day in the next few years. At that time, the woods were full of skeptics and hatchetmen, ardently hoping for the failure of the CBOE's "pilot market." New concepts, particularly in the financial field, are always greeted with scorn by the establishment. While I disavowed such pessimism because of my years of experience with options, my own enthusiasm was conservatively dampened. My judgment was overly restrained. Before 1975 had gone by the boards, trading volume had already reached 100,000 contracts on one day of unusual activity.

In 1978, the *average daily* trading *volume* on the CBOE alone exceeded 115,000 contracts per day, with one peak day exceeding 400,000 contracts. There can hardly be a doubt among reasonable people that the options industry has become a permanent adjunct to the realm of investment possibilities.

Yet, there have been problems, some real and some imagined.

Rather than some inherent fallacy with the options market, these difficulties are simply the natural growing pains of an industry that had come so far in so short a time.

The initial criticism leveled at options trading was that the activity seriously detracted from the capital formation function of the overall equity market. Money that would normally flow into new issues was instead being attracted to the listed "options action." Additionally, the fury of options trading was exerting a manipulative influence on the underlying common stock. These fears were most prevalent as options trading volume grew by leaps and bounds.

To address these issues, the CBOE sponsored a full-blown investigation by Robert R. Nathan Associates in 1974. The Nathan study did indeed uncover tie-ins between options and the underlying stock, but none so dire as predicted. Firstly, there was no evidence at all that options had been stealing the thunder of the new issue market. Secondly, options appeared to have some effect on the trading volume of the underlying stock, but there was no statistical evidence to indicate that they artificially influenced prices or volatility. On the contrary, they did seem to *increase stock trading volume* and *decrease* stock *volatility*. In a market dominated by the institutions, this improved liquidity is clearly a significant plus. More current studies are under way. The most recent evidence is not all in. It might well be that each new investigation will thoroughly delineate a condition which has long since ceased to exist. Such is often the case with a rapidly evolving new institution. Bureaucratic cannons frequently mistake shadows for substance.

Abstract issues begat concrete issues. The discovery of a few floor trading abuses prompted the SEC to request a voluntary moratorium on industry expansion in late 1977. This temporary respite also gave the agency some much-needed time to probe the significant regulatory problems. Puts had just started trading and their role in the total option scheme was very imperfectly understood. Several of the options exchanges had primitive trade tracking procedures and the commission concluded that an absolute audit trail was required. It wouldn't know if there were further trading abuses until a system was devised to detect them. And lastly, a few overzealous salesmen were gulling unsophisticated customers into visions of "wealth beyond their wildest dreams."

The Securities and Exchange Commission spent nearly two years considering these issues and trying to devise appropriate remedies. The commission has indicated that the moratorium should be lifted before the end of 1979.

At the onset of the moratorium, there were Call options available on 225 underlying stocks and twenty-five Puts. While there will undoubtedly be more underlying stocks added to the lists for Calls, by far the major expansion will come from Puts. Trading Calls without Puts on the stock is a two-legged stool. The maximum benefit will accrue to both speculators and investors alike when there is complete option symmetry to the underlying stock.

What does the future hold besides more Puts? I predict there will be an enormous expansion in both option trading volume and the number of market participants. It is estimated that the institutions are responsible for approximately 10 percent to 15 percent of the Call option volume. Yet, it is these same institutions which generate approximately 70 percent of the New York Stock Exchange volume. These institutions comprise the bank trust departments, insurance companies, corporate, union, and governmental pension and profit sharing plans. None of these entities has ever been characterized as impetuous.

Nonetheless, the wheel relentlessly turns. One by one, their interest will be piqued by the advantages of hedging with options. As a Call option seller, they can transfer part of their portfolio risk to a willing speculator. As a cash-secured Put seller, they can either buy stock at a discount or earn an enhanced return on their cash equivalents. With a nearly infinite number of strategic permutations at their disposal, they can easily adjust the risk-and-return characteristics of their holdings without the turmoil of all trying to go through either a "buy" or "sell" knothole at the same time.

Each year, the number of institutions working with options

grows to some degree. And as the bandwagon rolls on, the nonparticipants will begin to stir. After all, *consensus determines prudence.* As that consensus forms, considerations of prudence will become a spur, rather than a restraint, to the managers of these giant pools of securities. It is not at all inconceivable that, within less than a decade, a money manager will have to *defend* himself for *not* using options as a portfolio tool.

The culmination of the expansion will come with the introduction of options on government securities and Ginnie May Bond futures. Proposals for this expansion of options on debt instruments have already been made by several exchanges. It will only be a matter of time, and the time will be short.

In another age the impetus behind the options industry would have probably never developed. Innovation springs from need. The last decade has confronted the financial markets with more uncertainty and turmoil than we have seen in half a century—inflation fueled by federal policy, the energy crisis, the collapse of political credibility both at home and overseas, the enfeeblement of the economy by competing social goals and a terribly mismanaged tax structure, and the explosion of a bureaucracy bent on achieving anachronistic objectives. These are the diverse forces that have spawned the sudden burst of creativity in the investment community. Not surprisingly, the birth took place on LaSalle Street in Chicago, *not* on Wall Street in New York.

Both private and corporate investors fear uncertainty. *Rationality in an irrational world is terrifying.* If they can't change the world, they'll change their approach to dealing with it. Take quick profits. Cut losses even faster. Above all, be flexible. Go with the flow! Adapt! Hedge! And that's really what options are all about. They're a tool for survival.

Postscript

We'd rather take a dose of cod liver oil than admit a mistake. None of us feels perfect. Far from it. That's why mistakes hurt so badly. Because we're all groping along at the outer edges of our own fallibility, afraid that just one more blunder will tumble us over the brink to the pit below. The pit is where we each condemn the *others*, those faceless, mumbling masses of people who belong where they are because of their numbing sameness. Inarticulate, dull, foolish, making the same dumb mistakes over and over again, they threaten the feeling of our own unique, valuable individuality.

Humility, being in a perpetual state of tawdry disrepair, invariably yields to spite. The gambler blames the dice, the dealer, the cards, even his karma. The speculator blames his broker, the "insiders" who wait to pounce on his order and rip him off, again even his karma. Blame is never found in our own stall. It's always shoveled out into the yard for someone else to step in it.

I was convinced before I went down on the floor of the CBOE

as a market maker that I was headed for speculator's paradise. Instead of paying $60 in commissions for a ten-lot option trade, I would only have to pay $3.60. More importantly, when I wanted to buy contracts, I could just buy them myself. When I wanted to sell contracts, I could just sell them. No phone calls to make, no orders written, no waiting to learn if I had made the trade. I could do it all myself, instantaneously. There would be no one to blame but myself.

Before I tell you about paradise, let me briefly explain one pertinent fact of life about the options markets. Options are a derivative of the underlying stock. They have no meaning, no value that is independent of the common stock. Despite very temporary aberrations, the options follow the stock like a dog on a leash. And the leash is always in someone else's hand.

Speculators and professional traders alike are at the absolute mercy of the underlying stock's gyrations. The order flow from the public investors and institutions drives the price one way and then another throughout the day and through the year. Sometimes the price merely oscillates like a vibrating reed. Other times, and almost always unexpectedly, the price jumps around like popcorn in a popper.

The point is this: The principal difference between a shrewd speculator and the professional trader is that the latter is at risk every day to earn a living. If the professional trades with restraint and discipline, always keeping his position sized to the risk and his invested capital, he can make a respectable six-figure living. Even the best will take an occasional dumping. A $25,000 to $50,000 loss is not unusual if the stock gaps up or down on some unanticipated news. The successful trader doesn't choke. He reassesses his position and the condition of both the stock and the broad market. And then goes back to work. This is the only way to survive in a career built on virtually total uncertainty.

The killings you've either read or heard of come about from extraordinary risk coupled with superb luck. I personally know several men who each parlayed less than $50,000 to over

$3,000,000 in a year and a half. They were in "synch" with their karma and pyramided their luck into fortunes.

However, fate is remarkably evenhanded in dealing with her minions. Her net catches the greedy, the stubborn, the improvident, and the foolish. One man stayed at the game too long, stubbornly tried to defend his position in a contrary market, and lost every cent, including his original stake and then some. The other man wisely cashed in near the top of his move and actually enjoyed his wealth for months. But he couldn't resist the excitement of the "action." He had to trade, to keep taking shots in the hope of hitting again. In two years, he piddled his fortune away and had to leave the exchange floor.

The common denominator of these professional traders and the thousands of "failed" part-time speculators is plain greed. No man is immune to this monomaniacal impulse. It can be an overwhelming emotion. And as fatal as drunken driving.

Big money is made with big patience, which is easier said than done. Dramatic price moves are relatively rare. Patience has always been a singular virtue, but never more so than when trading options. A man who presses his luck is a man needlessly playing Russian roulette.

Recommended Trading Guidelines

During periods of enthusiasm, and corresponding periods of depression, many investors as well as professionals tend to either become enamored of their position or "freeze" at the decision-making point.

Consequently, I'd like to suggest some basic guidelines that can help in both establishing and liquidating options positions. Remember these are guidelines only and you may alter them to suit your own risk parameters. They can be a good discipline to prevent big profits from becoming losses or small losses from becoming disasters.

Prior to Buying Options Ask Yourself . . .

- Does the option offer the best leverage?
- Does the option offer limited risk?
- What is my objective on the stock (or option)?

With an Already Established Position . . .

- If an option declines 50 percent sell it.
- If an option increases 150 percent (from 2 to 5 for example), put in a mental stop order at 4 and move it up as the option moves up.
- Or, when an option increases 150 percent, sell one half the position and scale out on the balance.

Spreads—Bull/Bear

- If a spread goes against you by 50 percent, liquidate.
- If a spread is favorable by 100 percent, make a determination whether to liquidate or hold.

Ratio Spread

- Examine the spread for further action when the price of the stock hits the strike price of the short options. Do not adjust the spread by adding to the position.

Naked Option Writing

- If the option is unfavorable by 100 percent, repurchase it for a loss.
- If you establish a gain of 50 percent within 25 percent of the lifetime of the option, repurchase it for a profit.

Covered Option Writing

- If a stock declines by 10 percent, consider some alternatives: ratio writing (in suitable accounts), rolling down, rolling out to later maturity, or possible liquidation of the position.

Glossary

BETA An index measuring the sensitivity of a stock's price to overall fluctuations in the New York Stock Exchange's Composite Average. A beta of 1.5 indicates a stock tends to rise (or fall) 1.5 percent with a 1 percent rise (or fall) in the NYSE Composite Average.

BEAR SPREAD This is an options strategy designed to capitalize on a decline in the underlying stock. This strategy is applicable to both Puts and Calls. It consists of selling the lower strike price option and buying the higher strike price option with the same expiration.

BULL SPREAD This is an options strategy designed to capitalize on an advance in the underlying stock. The strategy is applicable to both Puts and Calls. It consists of buying the lower strike price option and selling the higher strike price option with the same expiration.

THE BUTTERFLY HEDGE   This hedge incorporates the underlying stock, an excess number of Calls sold against the stock, with the upside liability defined by the purchase of Calls at the higher strike price sufficient to balance the excess number of options sold. The strategy is neutral to moderately bullish depending upon the strike price of the options sold to the stock price.

THE BUTTERFLY SPREAD   This strategy is applicable to both Puts and Calls. It consists of buying the lower strike price option, selling twice as many of the next higher strike price option, and then buying the next higher strike price option in a number equal to the first lot bought. All options have the same expiration. In essence, this strategy is a combination of a bull spread and a bear spread. It is generally neutral in outlook, but can have either a bearish or bullish bias depending upon the price relationship between the underlying stock and the options sold, and whether Puts or Calls are employed.

CALL MONEY   Also, Call loans. Money lent by banks to brokers, collateralized by securities and subject to repayment upon demand.

CALL OPTION   A contract that entitles the owner to buy 100 shares of a stock at a stipulated price at any time during the period the option is in force.

COMBINATION   Any deployment of Puts and Calls held either long or short with different strike prices and expirations that is not otherwise denominated.

COVERING   Also, buying in. A term used to describe the completion of a short sale transaction whereby the stock is bought on the open market and used to replace those shares borrowed and originally sold short. Also refers to closing out a short option position.

DEBIT BALANCE   An accounting total that represents the total charges (i.e., money borrowed from the broker) against a customer's margin account.

DEBT LEVERAGE   The concept of borrowing money to buy securities. Any increase or decrease in the total value of the securities accrues to the borrower alone, not the lender.

DIAGONAL TIME SPREAD   A variation of the conventional time spread, the diagonal consists of selling a nearby at-the-money option and using the proceeds to buy a larger number of deferred options with a higher strike price.

EQUITY   The net value of an account after all money borrowed from the broker is subtracted from the market value of the securities in the account.

IN-THE-MONEY   A term used to describe an option that has intrinsic value. A Call at 40 on a stock trading at 50 is in-the-money 10 points.

INTRINSIC VALUE   A measure of the value of an option or a warrant if immediately exercised.

LONG   A person who owns stock either outright or in a margin account. Also used as an adjective to describe outright ownership.

MAINTENANCE MARGIN   The minimum amount of equity required in a margin account. The current maintenance margin is an equity equal to or greater than 30 percent of the account's market value. If the equity falls below this level, either more money must be put up or the stock sold out.

MARGIN   The term used to describe buying securities when a portion of the purchase price is borrowed from the brokerage house. Specifically, the margin is the amount of money that the customer must put up when buying on credit.

MARGIN CALL   The request by a broker for more money to bring a margin account up to the minimum maintenance margin requirement.

MARKET VALUE   The current value of all the securities held in a margin account.

NAKED CALL   A Call option originated by an option writer who does not own or buy the 100 shares of the stock on which the option is written, but rather leaves cash or other unencumbered equity in his account as a surety that he will honor his contract.

NAKED PUT   A Put option originated by an option writer who does not sell short 100 shares of the stock on which the option is written, but rather leaves cash or other unencumbered equity in his account as a surety that he will honor his contract.

OPTION BUYER   The person who buys Calls, Puts, or any combination thereof.

OPTION SELLER   Also, option writer. The person who originates an option contract by promising to perform a certain obligation in return for the price of his option.

OUT-OF-THE-MONEY   A term used to describe an option that has no intrinsic value. A Call at 40 on a stock trading at 30 is out-of-the-money 10 points.

PREMIUM   That portion of an option price that is in excess of the intrinsic value, if any. In cases where the strike price and the stock price are the same, the total cost of the option is premium.

PUT OPTION   The right to sell 100 shares of a security at a fixed price at any time during the option period.

RATIO HEDGE   Incorporates the underlying stock and selling more Call options than are covered by the stock. The number of options compared to the number of 100 share stock units constitutes the "ratio." The strategy is usually slightly bullish. The additional options sold provide additional downside protection, but also pose an upside risk should the stock advance sharply.

RATIO SPREAD   This strategy applies to both Puts and Calls. With Puts, it is moderately bearish. The Put ratio spread consists of buying the higher strike price options and selling a larger number of the lower strike price options, all with the same expiration. With Calls, this spread is moderately bullish. It consists of buying the lower strike price Calls and selling a larger number of the higher strike price Calls with the same expiration.

SEC   The Securities and Exchange Commission, a federal agency charged with regulating the securities industry.

SHORT   A person who has sold securities he doesn't own, and who consequently has an obligation to ultimately repurchase a like amount of shares on the open market. A person who sells an option in an opening transaction.

SHORT SALE   Selling stock one doesn't own in anticipation of repurchasing the borrowed stock at a lower price. Under current regulations, the shares sold short must first be borrowed.

SPREADS   In the OTC option market, a spread is a Put and a Call combination on the same stock with each option having a different strike price. In the listed market, a spread is a combination of buying a Call and writing a Call with a different strike price or expiration date option on the same stock. To qualify for spread margin treatment, the short option must expire at the same expiration or sooner than the long option.

STRADDLE   The combination of a Put and a Call on the same stock with each option having the same strike price and expiration.

STRIKE PRICE   The price at which an option can be exercised.

TIME SPREAD   Also known as the *Alligator*. Applicable to both Puts and Calls, the time spread consists of selling a nearby option and buying a more deferred option with the same strike price. This strategy is most effective when the underlying stock is relatively stable.

Index